Deaf in the Mind

The forgotten children
of Boston Spa

To Peter ;
Best Wishes
From Kevin

2012

Kevin Fitzgerald

A CIP catalogue record for this title is available from the British Library

ISBN: 978-0-9564756-0-2

Typeset by Andrew Searle

Front cover illustration and illustration opposite by Sue Wallace

Printed and bound in the UK by Anthony Rowe Ltd

KEVIN FITZGERALD
543 Oldham Road,
Middleton, Manchester, M24 2DH
Email: kevinfitz35@yahoo.co.uk

What matter deafness of the ear when the mind hears,
The one true deafness, the incurable deafness,
is deafness of the mind.

Victor Hugo

Acknowledgements

My heartfelt thanks go to Andy Searle, without whose help this book would never have happened.

Thanks to John Lawler for giving me the idea to write about St Johns, Boston Spa.

Love and thanks to my beautiful wife Diana for her patience and understanding and allowing me to spend countless hours pounding away at my keyboard.

Also, many thanks to Terry Riley and Rachael O'Neill for their help and advice.

Contents

About the author

KEVIN FITZGERALD'S LIFE STORY is a remarkable one. Profoundly deaf from the age of six after contracting meningitis, he spent eight years in an Institution for the Deaf and Dumb before entering a post-war world with little in the way of formal education.

After working as a cutter in a ladies' costume and mantle factory, he became a roofer, a job he did for 34 years despite his disability, which caused balance problems. In the 1990s he worked at the Royal Mail, where the culture of bullying of deaf workers, which he deduced was the result of communication problems, led him to go to college to become a highly qualified sign language teacher for the Open College of Sign Language (OCSL). He is now the Chief Examiner of OCSL.

In 1959, he married Diana, who had been profoundly deaf since birth, and they recently celebrated their 50th wedding anniversary. They have two daughters and a son, four grandchildren and four great grandchildren. The whole family lives in the Middleton area of Manchester.

Kevin has campaigned tirelessly for the end to discrimination for deaf people. ***Deafness of the Mind*** is his first book.

Foreword

I FELT HUMBLED when approached by Kevin to write this short foreword, and it got me thinking, not so much about Kevin but what his story is really about.

Kevin's story is written not with malice or anger, but with a passion to tell us how it was. Reading it I could not fail to be moved by his stubborn determination to prove he was a good as the next man, and even better. St John's Boston Spa has many happy memories for me through my dad, and I have visited and stayed many times. The camaraderie of the children lives from that tender age till one dies; it certainly did with my dad.

Yes, things were hard in those institutionalised environments, but Kevin brings it even more to the fore, along with those small anecdotes of what now we consider comical, but in those days was frowned upon and punished by the Sisters. Deaf education has come on a long way since those days, however. We all take education and our precious democracy for granted, yet without information, we are unable to make informed decision; without knowledge we cannot participate, and this, sadly, as Kevin tell us, is so prevalent in Deaf Education.

Be prepared to weep and smile as the story unfolds of an angry young man growing up and finding life, which could and should have been better. Kevin, like Martin Luther King, had a dream. I also had a dream and I told him, like Obama said, "Yes, we can!"

Terry Riley
Chairman, British Deaf Association

Introduction

ST JOHN'S INSTITUTION for the Deaf and Dumb has had, in its near 140-year history, well over 10,000 deaf inmates (I hesitate to call them students) pass through its portals. As far as I am aware no accurate account has ever been written about its history; hardly surprising when you consider that an estimated 90% of the deaf boys and girls left the Institution at the age of 16 unable to read or write. Students of Deaf History will search in vain for an accurate account.

Moreover, there is a glut of books about deafness and deaf issues written by hearing people, who cannot possibly know what it means to be deaf. This story, however, is written by me, Kevin Fitzgerald, and I am, myself, a deaf man and former inmate of St John's.

Like all the other inmates, I left St John's institutionalised and ill-equipped to face a life outside the institution. By dint of hard work and sacrifice I set about educating myself. I was shocked to find that I was banned from every further education class I tried to enrol at because of my deafness; the reason given was that I would hold the other students back. I would have given up in despair had not my younger sister, Patricia, decided to take my education upon herself. She taught me to read and write the Queen's English and to pronounce words correctly, and Patricia instilled in me a lifetime love of books and reading.

This story covers the years 1943 to 1951, when I was resident at St John's. Some of the things I have written about may shock, but it is a true account of one little boy's life in wartime and post-war Britain and the appalling education of deaf children in those far-off years of the 1940s and 1950s. It also describes what it was like to be institutionalised and then, at the tender age of 16, to be sent out into an alien world unable to hear, speak, read or write and with a head filled with religious dogma.

This book is dedicated to all those deaf children who passed through St John's and went through life unable to read or write the Queen's English. I have a feeling that the spirits of Billy Jones, Willie Kelly, John Wilson, Cyril Clarke and all those other deaf friends of mine who died untimely deaths are looking down and nodding their heads approvingly: Go for it Kev! Tell it like it was.

Kevin Fitzgerald, 2010

PART ONE

When I could hear

MY STORY BEGINS with one of my earliest memories, a memory of when I could make a bit of sense of what was happening around me. When I was five years old, on an Autumn night in 1940, my brother Jimmy, sister Patricia and myself were awakened by Mam shaking us and saying urgently, "Come on kids, wake up, the air raid siren is going again, we have to go down to the shelter."

"Oh Mam, let us stay in bed," we pleaded.

But Mam was adamant, "No, you must come to the shelter." As I rubbed the sleep from my eyes I could hear the boom of bombs exploding and when looking back, remembering that night, I marvel that we were able to sleep through it. Hitler's Luftwaffe bombers were on a raid over Manchester again, so leaving our warm, snug bed, we struggled into our clothes in the dark and went down to the communal air raid shelter accompanied by the eerie wailing of the air raid siren and some man who we couldn't see but could certainly hear. He was singing at the top of his drunken quavering voice:

Praise the Lord, and pass the ammunition!
Praise the Lord, and pass the ammunition!
Praise the Lord and pass the ammunition!
And the war will soon be over!

I suppose the bombing affected people in different ways. I can remember there was fear in that man's voice, and he seemed to be singing in tune with the wailing of the air raid siren. The tremulous uncertainty in that person's voice sent shivers running up and down my spine as it followed us across the street to where the air raid shelter was. Mam had made us put on our gas masks before we left the house and they would steam up from our breath, so it was hard to see where we were going, especially as there was a blackout on. I held on to my little sister Patricia to make sure that she didn't fall, and to let her know that I was looking after her and not to be frightened of the drunken man or the dark.

Alcoholism was rife in the poor working class areas of Manchester. I suppose it was an escape from the miserable working or family living conditions that many people had to endure, so many turned to alcohol to make their misery more bearable. Also, peer pressure, a fundamental way your friends affect your thoughts and behaviour, is powerful, but because it surrounds you, it is easy to overlook. For some people alcohol is just a means of relaxing, but for others it becomes an incurable disease and, once hooked, they are fighting it for the rest of their lives. Many just give in and throw their lives away in an alcoholic stupor. It is especially easy to give in to it when your country is under attack and you are frightened that your life could end at any moment. Film tough guys such as Humphrey Bogart were always knocking back slugs of bourbon and smoking cigarettes, so many people thought it was the cool thing to do in emergencies. Family, wives, children, friends, all can suffer from one person's addiction to alcohol. Addiction to nicotine seems to only affect the person concerned, whereas alcoholism affects whole families.

Our sleep had been interrupted like this by the bombing raids for the past few nights. Mam had put strips of sticky tape on the windows in a criss-cross pattern. Hopefully this would stop shards of glass flying into the room if a bomb blast was to blow the windows in. There were sheets of black paper tacked over the windows as well; the curtains were drawn every night to make sure that no glimmer of light showed outside. We had to make sure that all the lights were out before we opened the door and made our way to the air raid shelter in the dark, because the blackout was in force and the street lights, which were gas lights, had not been lit for a long time. Maybe the gas man, who came round at dusk to light them, had gone to join the army. I am sure that more people were killed in accidents caused by the blackout than were killed by the bombing. Sometimes we had to get up twice in a night and lack of sleep was beginning to tell on us. We were tired all the time and I for one could have easily slept right through the bombing if Mam had not woken us up. Our little Pat was beginning to get dark circles under her eyes and I was getting worried about her. I heard a woman saying that she thought that the man who operated the air raid siren was overly keen on his job. Many people were beginning to ignore the air raid siren now, or were just too tired to be bothered. All this talk made it hard for me to comprehend what was, in fact, real terror and death raining down on us from the German bombers.

Many men, my Dad included, couldn't be bothered to leave the pub to go to the shelter. I think that beer was rationed and they were only allowed two or three pints a night and they tried to make those few pints stretch as long as they could. They would go to the pub every night to make sure they had their full quota. They said that if your name is on the bomb then you couldn't do anything about it. It was many years before I finally understood what they meant by that fatalistic statement.

It was a dull, cloudy night with a hint of rain in the air as we hurried to the shelter. Hitler's bombers were directly overhead; they were flying high over Manchester coming in waves like swarms of wasps. The bombs made a strange whistling sound as they came down, ending in a mighty 'Ker- rump' that lit up the night sky as they exploded. This was followed by the crashing and clattering of bricks and stones and other things as the buildings collapsed. There was a funny coppery taste in my mouth and a strange feeling in my stomach as I ushered our Patricia down the steps into the air raid shelter, then I stood hesitating at the entrance, looking around at the beams from the searchlights criss-crossing the night sky searching for enemy bombers. Even at that early age I knew that this was not good and that it was dangerous. I had no concept of what death meant, but I knew what it was like to be hurt. Only the other day I had tripped on the pavement and hurt myself, so in my childish mind I was thinking that these bombs would hurt me, only more so than tripping on the pavement did.

The air raid shelters were dug deep into the ground, lined with brick walls three bricks thick and capped with thick slabs of reinforced concrete. They seemed to me to be quite roomy inside, but then I was only a little kid and didn't take up much space. There were rows of bunks three tiers high along two walls.

Silver barrage balloons were dotted like ghostly sentinels across the night sky. Across the street there was a small red shale playground adjacent to Willert Street police station. Sometimes, in happier times, we would take bottles of water and jam butties to this little park and picnic while we watched the home guard on manoeuvres. Some of them had twigs and leaves stuck in their hats, which I was told made them invisible to the enemy. As a little kid, I always imagined that our soldiers were a fearsome lot of ruthless killers that would strike terror into the hearts of any German soldiers foolish enough to tangle with them. Many years in the future I would be reminded of this scene when watching 'Dads' Army' on the television.

The metal railings that once had surrounded the park had gone to be melted down to help the war effort, and people were giving any old pans and other metal objects to help. Some kids were going round the neighbourhood knocking on doors and asking for any unwanted metal pans etc., and taking them to the scrap yard in home-made carts. It was such a precious commodity, every little bit helped, and some kids were even giving their precious pieces of shrapnel. It was good to know that you were doing your bit to help your country in times of trouble. Once there had been swings, a seesaw, slide, roundabout and a sand pit for the local children to play with, but not any more; they had all been taken away too. Instead, there was at one end of the playground a barrage balloon station and in the middle was a searchlight placement surrounded by a wall of sandbags. The anti-aircraft guns that were situated in Heaton Park about two miles away were shooting up shells as fast as they could at a German bomber that was caught in the glare of several searchlight beams that were converged on it.

My mind was absorbing everything that was happening. It would be imprinted their, never to be forgotten. I have often cast my mind back to that scene and I can recall every detail of the German bomber caught in the glare, and the ack ack shells bursting all round it. It was so exciting to my five year old mind and gave a strange feeling of fear that made my belly feel queasy.

Suddenly, a massive hand was on my head. I turned to see Mr Willis, a neighbour from the bottom flat. Mr Willis was a big, ruddy-faced, red-haired man who worked as a hod carrier for the bricklayers, some of whom were women brickies because there was a shortage of men as they were in the armed forces. They were building flats in Collyhurst before the bombing started. "Kevin me lad," he said kindly, "I think ye'd best get thyself inside, thee might get hurt, there's a lot of shrapnel flying about tonight." Shrapnel was like currency among the kids of the locality. If I could find a piece about six inches long I could swap it for a patched up leather case ball. I nodded my head. Mr Willis was right; only the air raid wardens were walking about on a night like this, making sure that not a chink of light was showing from the windows to give the Germans a target at which to aim their bombs. I thought to myself that I would search for shrapnel tomorrow when the raid was over, so with a last look around I turned and went down the steps into the shelter to rejoin my Mam, big brother Jimmy and little sister Patricia. So I never saw if the German bomber was shot down and I have often wondered if it made it home safely.

The only illumination in the air raid shelter came from a few candles. There were some electric lights, but they were either broken or not connected up. The people would pass the time by playing guessing games, telling stories, or singing. I remember well one night in the air raid shelter when all us kids were tired and half asleep and all the adults were in a sombre mood. I could feel there was a lot of sadness in the air. One woman started to sing in a very low, mournful voice, and slowly others began to join in and the crescendo built up until all the grown ups were singing:

> *Keep the home fires burning*
> *While your heart is yearning*
> *Though your lads are far away*
> *They dream of home*
> *There's a silver lining*
> *Through the dark clouds shining*
> *Turn the dark clouds inside out*
> *Til' the boys come home*

Some of the adults were openly crying, with tears streaming down their faces; it was a very disconcerting sight for us kids to see the adults being so sad as we couldn't understand why, we were far too young to really understand the horrors of war. Maybe the older kids understood, but us little ones were far too young to know what was going on, which in a way was a good thing. We knew that war was a bad thing and Hitler was a 'Baddie'. I remember having a funny feeling in my belly when the bombs were coming down, but, on the whole, I looked on it as an adventure and we were living in exciting times. I suppose you could call it 'the confidence (or ignorance) of youth'.

Mam was sitting on the bench with Jimmy on one side of her and me on the other side and Patricia on her lap. She had her arms around us and we could feel her sadness. Those were such extraordinary and deeply emotional times that almost 70 years later I can still remember how emotionally charged the air was in that air raid shelter all those years ago. I now understand how futile war is; it never solves anything that talking can't do better. It only causes heartbreak for ordinary people, most of whom don't even know what they are fighting for, and even if they did know I doubt if they would think it was worth fighting or dying for. Why not let the posh people or politicians, or whoever started the wars, fight it out themselves. These people had stolen the lives of many women and children and fine brave young men. I'm talking about the German people as well as the British people. Manchester City's goalkeeping legend Bert Trautmann is a fine example of what the ordinary German's temperament is like. Propaganda is a powerful weapon, especially in the hands of a powerful orator. The British were told that God is on our side and we were fighting for freedom; the Germans were told exactly the same thing, (Gott Mit Uns), but those are just my thoughts.

My Dad had been working as a cooper all day and the interrupted sleep of the past few nights had made him very tired, so instead of coming into the shelter with us, he went to the pub for a couple of pints to help him to sleep. All his pals must have been tired too because they were all in the pub as well. My dad would say that a couple of pints of Chester's mild is better than a sleeping tablet.

My Dad's name was Jimmy. He was of medium height and he was a cooper by trade. He made barrels from oak wood and this had given him a wiry build, with large sinewy hands, and he was deceptively strong for his size. Once, when some men were having a competition to see who could get one of the big barrels of beer and stand it up from a lying position, after these men had failed my Dad just walked up to them, moved some out of the way, grasped the barrel, and, with a slight rocking movement, had it standing up in no time at all.

My Mam was a small woman and, like most of my aunties, she had long red hair, Mam's name was Ellen, but to us she was just "Mam." My brother was named Jimmy too, he was two years older than me and he was covered in freckles. My sister Patricia was two years younger than me and she was a very pretty little blue eyed blonde and I adored her. I was the middle child and I was blonde and blue-eyed too.

Isn't it odd the way some seemingly trivial happening or words will remain in your mind? If you take stock of your memories what a hotchpotch of recollections they will present, so I remember this conversation with Ken, one of my friends of the same age.

"Where have you been Kev? I was looking all over for you before," he said.

"Oh! Just looking at the Jerry bombers," I said with a shrug,

"Oooh! Kev, you could have been killed."

I gave him a contemptuous look and thought, 'What a Jessie'. I was feeling very tired and these German bombing raids were becoming a nightly occurrence, so I turned away to find a bunk. I was going to sleep on a bottom bunk with my little sister. Ken followed me over and said:

"Kev, it's best to sleep in the top bunk 'cos the bombs always come down on the slant and land in the bottom bunks."

At five years of age that made sense, so I said, "Thanks Ken." I woke Patricia up and we climbed into the top bunk. I was very protective of our Patricia and I thought that this move might possibly save our lives, so Ken can't be so bad then. After that we were good friends, not 'best friends', as that title was reserved for Barney Conrad, whom I had recently met when I had started proper school, not nursery school.

My school was St Malachi's, and because it was war time and clothes were rationed, we didn't have to wear a uniform. Most of us were dressed in patched up clothes and I always wore my brother Jimmy's hand-me-downs. Mam always bought our clothes too large from the clothing club so that we would grow into them. When Jimmy grew out of his clothes, they were passed down to me. It must have been very hard for mothers to keep their children in shoes and clothes because we seemed to outgrow them in a matter of weeks. My Mam also bought us clogs from a shop opposite the 'Playhouse', a cinema on Queens Road. The clogs had rubbers on the soles, but we would ask Dad to take the rubbers off and put steel ones on so that we could make sparks when we kicked them on the cobbles, and the steel ones were better for sliding on the ice. In the summer most of us went out to play in our bare feet to save our shoes or clogs for the winter. Our feet soon hardened and it was uncomfortable to wear shoes again when it became too cold to be barefooted.

There were posters on some walls with the legend 'Make do and Mend', with instructions on how to save materials such as cloth and paper. We would make go-carts out of old boxes and pram wheels. It wasn't until we were going downhill at breakneck speed that we realised we should have made some kind of braking system for them. So we kids were into 'make do and mend' and recycling as well. I suppose that we had to put up with things like that because toys were unobtainable. Also, like nearly everything else, clothes were rationed and as I was the smallest boy Jimmy's clothes had to do. In the neighbourhood gang I was "Little Fitz" and Jimmy was "Big Fitz". Mam was performing miracles keeping us fed on the wartime rations, nothing was ever wasted, not even stale bread. Mam could make it into a very tasty bread and butter pudding, but as butter was virtually unobtainable she used margarine instead. I have never seen bread and butter pudding since wartime, and most people seem to have never heard of it.

My pal Barney was very little; he only came up to my shoulder and I was small for my age too, but I was sturdily built, whereas Barney was diminutive. He was really small. I think he attached himself to me for protection. We went everywhere together and played together all the time. His Dad was away most of the time in the RAF. I often gave him a piggy back rides home when he became too tired to keep up with me. We were friends right up to when I was sent away to St John's Institution for the Deaf and Dumb [sic] in Boston Spa, Yorkshire and I lost touch with all my schoolmates.

There were a lot of German bombing raids on Manchester in the early years of the war. A raid that particularly stands out in my memory happened just before Christmas of 1940. As we were being hurried to the air raid shelter by Mam, I noticed the skies over Manchester were glowing red from the buildings that were on fire and I could hear the whistling sound of the bombs coming down and exploding and lighting up the sky, as well as dropping high explosive bombs, the Germans were also dropping thousands of incendiary bombs that were starting fires all over Manchester. The explosions were getting nearer and nearer, so no messing about this time, straight down into the shelter and hope that we will come out again alive once more when it was all over. This time there was no all-clear siren, the bombing continued all night. We could hear the odd brick or pieces of shrapnel hitting the air raid shelter and ricocheting off into the night and the pieces of shell from the ack ack guns that had exploded high up in the sky amongst the German bombers were also falling back down on us, so we were in the safest place. It would take a direct hit from a bomb on the air raid shelter to kill us. We lived near the railway tracks, so I think that the German bombers were aiming their bombs at the sparks from the trains. Despite the bombs falling all around us and the earth shaking from the explosions I fell asleep, so I never heard the all-clear going in the early hours of next morning.

Many years later, when I read other peoples accounts of what happened during the Manchester blitz, people say that the children were evacuated to places of safety in the countryside. I have no memory of being evacuated and I often wonder why the children of Collyhurst were not evacuated, but I don't think that many of us would have been too happy to leave our families to go and live with strangers. After what we were living through here, living in the country would be very boring.

Every afternoon we were marched from St Malachi's school to the Civic Hall on Churnet St. This was situated on the opposite side of the little park from Willert Street police station. The long orderly crocodile of school children, with their gas masks contained in cardboard boxes which were hung round their necks with string, walked down the street in the care of two teachers whose names I have long forgotten. We were arranged in order of age and classroom. Some of the bigger kids were chanting over and over as we marched, "Whistle while you work! Hitler is a twerp! He wiped his bum with bubble gum! And stuck it to his shirt!" There were many little made up songs like that; they were encouraged because it was thought to keep the kids' morale up.

In the Civic Hall we sat on wooden benches at long wooden tables and were given a dinner. The dinner usually consisted of lots of potatoes, cabbage that was boiled into submission and rock hard peas, all covered in a gravy made from Oxo, which provided the meat flavour. Sometimes when we had a slice of fried spam you could hear the kids shouting, 'Yippee! Its spam fritters whooo!' This was usually followed by a pudding of semolina or sago, or sometimes when we were lucky we would have stewed apples and custard. The apples were dried apples that had been soaked in water overnight to reconstitute them and the custard was made from dried milk. Still, to us kids they were delicious, and anyway, beggars can't be choosers! A favourite of mine was dried egg when it was available, the dried egg powder maling delicious omelettes. The bombing and lack of sleep didn't seem to have affected my appetite and I would eat whatever was put in front of me. Oranges and bananas were a thing of the past. I could vaguely remember having a banana when I was a toddler, but I couldn't remember what they tasted like and it would be six years before I tasted another. Mam would get bottles of rosehip syrup from the clinic to give us our daily dose of vitamin C and castor oil, which was horrible but Mam said it was good for us. I suspect that this dinner at the Churnet Street Civic Hall was the only nourishment that a lot of the kids received for the day. Still, it is amazing what you can put up with when you have no choice.

I was born in Naylor Street, Miles Platting, a predominantly Irish neighbourhood in one of the rougher parts of North Manchester. It is now called the 'Northern Quarter' and houses there cost a small fortune, but in those days the houses consisted of rows and rows of two-up two-down terraces, back-to-back with the toilet in the tiny back yard and narrow ginnels between them. My Dad was of Irish extract and he had many brothers and sisters, of which he was the youngest. My Mam's family was of Welsh extract, from that massive Welsh clan the Williams'. She was also the youngest of a large family. I have a vague memory of living in a little terraced house which was kept spotlessly clean, not just inside the house but the pavement outside as well, where the stone front steps and most of the pavement were donkey-stoned daily by a little old lady who always wore a long black dress, a long black shawl over her head and shoulders and had clogs on her feet that would click- clack on the cobbles when she walked. I learned later after she had died that she was my Granny Fitz. I was only a toddler when she died so I can't remember forming any kind of relationship with her and my Granddad died in 1917, so I never really had any Grandparents.

We moved to number 40 Northern Drive, Collyhurst in 1938 or 1939, I'm not sure exactly when. Manchester Corporation began the house-clearing programme before the war. They built the new flats to house the people from the clearances of Miles Platting. However, the war came along and put a stop to all that; Herman Göring's Luftwaffe helped to clear a lot of the Manchester slums anyway.

After the air raids of the previous night we were fuzzy-headed from lack of sleep when we woke up next morning. Mam gave us a breakfast of porridge, washed our hands and faces, made sure that Jimmy and me had our gas masks and packed us off to school. Patricia had her Mickey Mouse gas mask and our next door neighbour, Mrs Hibbert, looked after her while Mam went to her part time job at the Acme Tin Stamping Company, which was just across the road and made tin hats and cooking utensils for the soldiers and sailors. That was my mum's contribution to the war effort.

On the way to school someone told us that a bomb had landed on the air raid shelter in Hewart Road and had killed some people and injured some more. I said, "Bloody 'ell, that's where Barney lives" and dashed off to see if he was alright. Of course, many other people had been killed and their homes flattened, but to me Only Barney's air raid shelter seemed to matter, all the rest of it was too much for me to take in. I had to stop and see the damage that the bombs had done the previous night and collect pieces of shrapnel that littered the streets. There were some big craters in the road and there was a big one right next to the air raid shelter; bricks and concrete lumps were scattered about all over the place and the windows in all the surrounding houses were shattered. The thick reinforced concrete roof on the bomb shelter had a big crack in it and part of it was hanging off. I could see the steel reinforcing bars, the entrance had been blown away but the shelter itself had withstood the bomb blast. There was a burst water pipe nearby and water was shooting high up into the air and one bomb crater had been turned into a lake from a burst mains pipe. There was a very unpleasant smell permeating the neighbourhood from where the blast of a bomb had ruptured the gas mains and from all the smouldering ruins. We were told that two people had been killed outright and lots more were injured, but luckily Barney was alright.

My uncle, Dick Fitzgerald, and his family lived near where the bombs had landed, but fortunately they were in another air raid shelter. My Mam's brother, uncle Dick Williams, and his family (lots of Dicks in our family) lived in nearby Kingsley Crescent too and they were also safe. There were lots of kids whooping and jumping about, full of excitement; school was forgotten, it was bedlam. The police and the ARP (Air Raid Precautions) wardens couldn't stop kids from running inside the bombed ruins looking for pieces of shrapnel and other things too. Maybe we were too young to understand the danger. The local cinema on Collyhurst Street was showing 'The Wizard of Oz' and to us kids the 'Wicked Witch of the West' was far more dangerous than Hitler. In fact, only the other day, when our cousin Winnie had taken Jimmy, Patricia and myself to see it, the Wicked Witch, with her green face, big hook nose and evil laugh ("Heh, heh, heh"), had so frightened me that under the pretext of going to the toilet I got up, left the Picture House and ran all the way home. When Winnie, Jimmy and Patricia came home they asked me why I had left the pictures. I said that I was bored with it and it was a daft film. I didn't want our Pat to know that the evil witch had scared me!

Because most fathers and big brothers were away in the forces, there was not much discipline amongst the kids and some of them were running wild and their Mams couldn't do anything with them. Some kids even had bullets which they had stolen from their dads, big brothers or uncles who were in the army. We would wedge the bullet between bricks and bang it with another brick and a nail until, with a bang, the bullet would shoot out. There were some kids who even had bayonets which they carried about and badges from all the various regiments. All these things were swapped and bartered, and some kids had quite a collection. It's no wonder that the police never patrolled the streets of Collyhurst alone; they were always in twos or threes. If the Germans had ever succeeded in invading Britain they would have been best advised not come to Collyhurst as they would have soon regretted it if they did.

One morning when we entered the classroom the teacher told us that one of our classmates from St Malachi's, a boy whose name I cannot remember, had been killed in an accident in his home. She didn't say what the accident was, or how he had been killed, but we found out later that he had thrown a bullet on the fire in his house and it exploded and shot into his mouth, killing him instantly. She made us all kneel besides our desks and say a prayer for him and ask Jesus to look after him in Heaven. After that, if any kid was absent the teacher would ask the one who lived nearest to call on the way home to see if they were still alive. Mostly the absentees were just playing truant.

Some things or happenings do seem to stick in your memory for no particular reason. I remember on the way home after school one day Barney and I were on an imagined raid into Germany. I would stop on the street corner, wave Barney back and whisper, "Shhh! Nazi's are there". Then I would take a hand grenade (imaginary), pull the pin out with my teeth and throw it round the corner. I would then peek round the corner and wave Barney over. "Got 'em Barney, we can go on now." Then, as we turned the corner we saw some workmen who had a big pot of pitch with a fire underneath it. We forgot that we were on a raid to kill Nazis in Germany. We stopped and squatted down on our haunches to watch them repairing the granite setts in Churnet Street. At that time most of the streets of Manchester we were lined with these granite setts. They were not cobble stones as most people seem to think, cobble stones were from an earlier age. I know that now because one of the workmen told me. Anyway, we were squatting there watching the workmen laying the setts. They had a bucket of hot pitch and would dip a sett in it and lay it in place. When they had filled in a square yard or so they would pour hot pitch between the gaps in the setts; we found it fascinating. We were asking the workmen questions and we must have been bothersome to them, but they were very patient with us.

"Hey! Mister, does it hurt if you get some of that black stuff on your hand?"

"Yes! Not arf it does kid."

"Do you get lots of money for doing that Mister."

"Yes! Cartloads."

"It stinks doesn't it mister!"

"No, it's good for your lungs."

"What are your lungs mister?"

"Your lungs are what you breathe with."

"What are you chewing mister? Is it chewing gum? Can I have some?"

"No, it's not chewing gum, it's pitch. Here, have some, you can chew it but don't swallow it or it will plug your bum up and then you can't shit."

He handed me a small piece of pitch and I put it gingerly in my mouth and bit down on it. It was hard at first, but gradually softened with the warmth from my mouth so I could chew on it just like chewing gum. Just then some kids came running towards us shouting excitedly, "The Acme's on fire! The Acme's on fiiiyer!"

I looked over in the direction of the Acme and, sure enough, there was a pall of black smoke billowing up into the air, so I shouted, "Come on Barney, let's go and have a look" and we dashed towards it.

As we were running, Barney said, "Is your Mam working now?"

"No, she finished her shift about two hours ago."

When we got there the fire engines were already there and there was a big crowd gathered to watch. The firemen had rigged up their hoses and dropped one end of it in a big concrete water tank that was situated on the croft just a few yards away. They must have been expecting something like this to happen and they built the concrete emergency water tank for just such an eventuality. These big concrete emergency water tanks had been built near most important buildings. Two of the firemen broke down a door with their axes and while one fireman used his hose to send streams of water through the open doorway, the other one went inside the building. I said to Barney "Wow! If they gotta do dat den I fink I'm not gonna be one." Barney said, "Me either." Don't forget, we were only kids and had not yet mastered the Queen's English, but we understood each other alright.

Eventually the fireman emerged from the smoke and fire carrying a man over his shoulder; the man was kicking and struggling and shouting, "Me mate's in there, lemme go, me mate's in there, I've gotta get 'im". Another fireman went to help. He pulled the struggling man off the first fireman and carried him some yards away. Just then the roof of the Acme collapsed and a shower of sparks and flames shot up into the sky. The man who had been rescued burst into tears and collapsed onto the ground. The fireman put his arm round him and gave him a cigarette and a woman from a nearby house gave him a cup of tea. The cup was shaking in his hands and slopping tea all over him; he was so shocked, poor fellow, his face was black from the smoke and his eyes were white, in contrast to his blackened face. His eyes were wild and staring with shock. I could see that he really wanted to go into the blazing inferno for his mate. There were a group of workers from the Acme who had got out in time. They were all clustered together talking agitatedly; it made me think – would I dash into a blazing building to save Barney? I decided no, I didn't think so, but better not tell him that. There was some talk that it was sabotage, but I didn't know what that word meant until much later when I asked my Dad. He told me that it meant that someone had done it on purpose to help Hitler. Now why on earth would anybody want to do that? I just couldn't understand it. Dad explained that it was all to do with politics, but that explanation still left me in the dark. When I saw Barney the next day I explained it to him. I said, "It wuz 'Ickler's pal who did it."

Most weekends we were at my Auntie Ruth's. She was one of Mam's flame-haired sisters. She lived down the road at Kingsley Crescent with Uncle Frank, who wore glasses that looked like the bottom of bottles and always had a pipe in his mouth, along with their two sons Frank and Joe. Cousin Frank was in the Black Watch and Cousin Joe was a couple of years older than Jimmy and me, but he always looked sickly and unhealthy. Auntie Ruth always seemed to have plenty of everything, even in these times of rationing she was never without coal, bread, beer, meat or cigarettes. The food shortage had not really begun to bite this early in the war – later on it would get much worse – but even then there were no pudgy kids like there are today.

Aunty Ruth always seemed to have a glass of beer in her hand and a cigarette in her mouth and she always greeted me in a very raspy voice, "Hello Kevin Dearie, do you want a butty?" Uncle Frank was always puffing away at his pipe; the front room of their house was always full of tobacco smoke and the walls were yellow with nicotine, so it really wasn't surprising that Joe always looked sickly. All the grown ups in our family smoked and drank. It seemed to be the way of life back then, you had to smoke and drink to show that you were grown up. It was a proud day when you reached your eighteenth birthday and you could openly go in the pub with your Dad and have a cigarette and a pint with him and it was all legal. Of all the grown ups only Mam didn't smoke. Of course, at that time nobody knew how deadly those habits were. Looking back with the benefit of hindsight, I marvel at the extent of the ignorance and false information that the average working man held; in fact, there was one brand of cigarette that was advertised, 'For your throat's sake smoke Craven A', and to roll your own cigarettes in brown liquorice paper was thought to be good for your bowels.

At the weekly gatherings at Auntie Ruth's we would eat until we were stuffed full. A favourite of mine was dripping butties. I was a very active little lad and I found it very hard to sit still. I'm sure a lot of my energy came from those dripping butties. This was wartime, don't forget, and rationing was in force. It never entered my mind to wonder where Auntie Ruth got all this stuff from. She was never tight with it either; she always gave us some if we were short. Many times my Mam would say, "Kevin, we're running out of sugar, be a good lad and go to Auntie Ruth's for some." At that time I knew nothing about Black Markets, 'under the counter' or 'spivs' and the fiddles that they got up to. My Auntie Ruth was the last person you would suspect of being involved in anything shady, but she knew some very dodgy characters.

There were crates of beer, spam sandwiches and sausage rolls too, and lots of different soft drink bottles. Now, when looking back to those long gone war years, I find it amazing that Auntie Ruth was able to get all these things and I often wonder how she did it. She was certainly a survivor. When all the grown ups had a drink and a cigarette in their hands and us kids had a lemonade or Tizer or Dandelion and Burdock, which was my favourite because it was the same colour as the beer that the grown ups were drinking, Auntie Ruth would sit at the piano and cousin Frank would get his accordion down from the top cupboard, and sometimes my Dad would get his rickers out of his pocket, and we would have 'sing-songs'. And so, in that snug and smoky atmosphere we would make our own entertainment.

Just in case you don't know I should explain that rickers were two flat pieces of bone about six inches long by two inches wide, shaped rather like shoe horns. You held them between the fingers of one hand and clicked them. They make a pleasant rhythmic sound and they were quite common during those days, but I have never seen or heard any one mention them since my childhood in Collyhurst. Most people seem to have heard of playing musical spoons, but not rickers. Maybe the word rickers is just a Manchester word, or maybe it is because I now live mainly in the deaf world that I haven't heard of them.

Cousin Frank would pick me up from under the table, where I usually was when I was chewing on my dripping butties, and he would plonk me down on the table and say, "Quiet!! Listen everybody, our little Kev is going to sing for his supper." I didn't need any prompting. I had a lovely singing voice then, or so I liked to think. I sang 'White cliffs of Dover', 'I'll take you home again Kathleen', 'When they sound the last all clear' and 'Hello Patsy Fagan', which was my dad's favourite and I always had to sing it for him. Also, a song called 'Der Fuhrer's face' (which he had taught me, but that one had some rather naughty words and it wasn't to be sung in mixed company), 'Silent Night', 'Away in a manger' and all the popular songs of the day, to the accompaniment of Auntie Ruth's piano and Cousin Frank's accordion and Dad's rickers. Those songs I can still remember to this day. When the adults had drunk all the beer, Uncle Frank and my Dad would go to the pub called The Salvage, which was just round the corner, and get a couple more crates of beer.

I had a cousin called Tommy who was the same age as me. His Mam was my auntie Mary, who was one of my Mam's sisters. They would be at my Auntie Ruth's too and Tommy would sing as well. Sometimes he would join me and we would sing a duet. Sometimes Tommy would come to our house for a sleepover and sometimes I would go to his house for a sleepover. Tommy's Dad was a coal miner and worked at Bradford pit on Grey Mare Lane. When I slept at Tommy's house I could see how tired his Dad was, it must have been very hard working in the mines. Tommy didn't follow his Dad into the mining industry when he left school, he became a plumber instead. I thought that was a very wise move because he was a bit of a mardy and not as tough as me. He didn't know about the 'Wizard of Oz' episode thankfully!

Tommy had an older sister whose name was Elsie. I thought she was lovely. I wasn't in love with her, but for some reason that I couldn't explain I would always do what she told me to do. She was always happy and smiling. She was a very happy person to be around and it was infectious, she made me happy too. When she was going out with her boyfriend she would paint her legs with a light brown substance (I'm not sure what it was, it could have been cold tea or gravy browning), and then she would ask me to help her to draw a black line down the back of her legs. The end result was that she looked as if she had nylon stockings on, very ingenious. Nylon stockings were very hard to get during the war. You could only get them on the black market. Auntie Ruth never bothered with stuff like that, only the basics like food etc. If you had an American boyfriend you could get nylons, the Americans always had plenty of things like that. It's no wonder they were so popular with the women! Unlike the British soldiers, the American GIs had lots of things and they were always very generous with them, but that didn't make them very popular with the British Tommies. There was a saying at the time that the Americans were, 'Over paid, over sexed and over here'.

We would make our way home through the blackout. The street lights were all out and it was pitch dark, but we had little pocket torches and we were given strict instructions that they must be pointed to the ground at all times; if you pointed it up the German bombers would know where you were and bomb you! When it was foggy it was difficult to see your own hand in front of your face. Everybody had coal fires then, and there were factory chimneys and those dark satanic mill chimneys spewing thick, black smoke out as well, so when the smoke and fog mixed you had a mixture of smoke and fog that was called smog, and that killed many people because of bronchitis and other breathing problems. On some occasions the smog was so dense that it would turn day into night; they called that type of fog a 'peasouper' because there was a greenish tinge to it. I think it was from sulphur in the smoke. Even though we had to breathe this sooty, sulphurous air lots of people still smoked cigarettes. It is such a strong addictive drug. I have seen some people with scarves wrapped around their sore throats, clutching their throats in agony, they could barely speak but still they tried to inhale the cigarette smoke, ostensibly to 'bring up the phlegm'. There were no cigarette butts on the streets because the down and outs would scour the streets searching for them. They would empty the tobacco into a tin and roll it into cigarettes. That was disgusting and showed how desperate some people were for tobacco, yet the big tobacco companies were allowed to sell it. It would be unthinkable today. All the buildings and houses were black and grimy and dismal looking and there was not a blade of grass to be seen anywhere, unlike the Collyhurst of today. Now there are trees, grass and flowers, and unlike when I was growing up there in the 1940s, you can actually see the Pennine hills from some vantage points.

My Mam came from a massive family, so did my dad, so I had lots of Aunties and Uncles and Cousins. One of my Dad's sisters, Auntie Mary, and her husband, Uncle George, had a farm in Newhey, which was up on the hills above Oldham. They would sometimes visit us on their motorbike, which had a sidecar attached, and sometimes they would have chickens and eggs in it for us. Dad came home one Saturday with a live chicken under his coat. Jimmy, Pat and I were excited to have a new pet! Mam gave me some money to take Patricia to the pictures and when we came home there was a lovely smell of roasting chicken wafting around the house. Patricia and I cried and were inconsolable, but when Mam served dinner we tucked in with gusto – kids are strange little creatures!

Family gatherings were a regular feature of my childhood, but at this time many uncles and cousins were unable to attend. Cousin Richard Fitzgerald was somewhere in Europe fighting the Nazis. He was later to be captured by the Germans at Arnhem. Uncle Andy McVey was in the merchant navy and his ship was later torpedoed and he was badly burned by blazing oil. He and his mates were in a rubber raft for a few days before they were rescued and he had to be invalided out of the merchant navy. Cousin George was in the Chindits in the Far East fighting the Japs in the jungle. There were more cousins and uncles in the forces but I don't know much about them. There were many families in Collyhurst who could tell similar stories. Those dark war years were hard on many families and Britain owes them a huge debt of gratitude. One of my Mam's brothers, Uncle Dick Williams, lived nearby. He was rather small and stocky and had been in the 'Manchester Pals' regiment in the First World War, fighting in the trenches. It must have been a terrifying experience, but he never talked about it. He had three children, Terry, Norma and Mona. I have lots of cousins all over Manchester and I am sorry that we never kept in touch with each other. Another Cousin, Anthony Williams, was famous. Family legend said that Anthony played football for Manchester United when their ground was at Newton Heath He was always called Anthony, not Tony, because of his exalted status.

Another family legend, this time on my Dad's side, was that one of my Dad's uncles was involved in the Manchester martyrs fiasco in which a group of Irishmen shot a policeman while trying to rescue some of their Fenian friends. Three of them were captured and were duly hanged at Strangeways prison; the rest of the fenians had to flee to America to avoid capture. After some years, and by growing a beard, my Dad's uncle was able to come back home.

Two of my Dad's brothers, Uncle Dick and Uncle Frank, lived nearby. Sometimes when Uncle Frank's wife had kicked him out he would come and stay at our house for a few days, until his wife would forgive him for whatever he had done and take him back again. I had the impression that my Mam didn't like them much but tolerated them for my Dad's sake. I should mention here that my Dad's brothers were coopers too; it was a trade that was passed down in my Dad's family. The reason why Jimmy and I were not coopers was because my Dad said it was a dying trade, and when the metal containers replaced the wooden barrels he was proved right. On the occasions when Uncle Frank was staying with us, Uncle Dick, Uncle Frank and my Dad would get together at our house and, after we had all gone to bed, they would stay up. After producing a bottle of what they called 'The Creature' (which they pronounced 'Crayture'), which would loosen their tongues, they would talk into the small hours, passing 'The Crayture' round and swigging from it. I would be listening at the door, which I would have opened a crack. It's funny that our Jimmy never had the same strong curiosity as I to know what was happening in our environment. Maybe he was just more laid back than me and I was just nosier, or maybe those dripping butties made me hyperactive. He and our Patricia were fast asleep in bed while I was at the door listening to my Dad, Uncle Dick and Uncle Frank talking about them Black and Tan 'Bastids' and the Fenian freedom fighters

I found out many years later that 'The Creature' was 'Poteen', which is a very potent illegal home-made alcoholic distillation. Uncle Dick made it in his backyard.

My Uncle Dick, who was the eldest brother, had two sons and two daughters. The eldest son was named Richard, like his Dad; next was Johnny, who was not much older than Jimmy and me, and Winnie was the same age as our Jimmy. The other daughter was named Margaret. I never knew her because she died at the age of sixteen when I was only about two years old. My Mam told me that when the war was over in 1945 Richard came home for a few days leave and one day he said that he had to go to a certain hotel in Manchester, I think it was the Midland Hotel, to meet one of the army VIPs. Richard went to keep that rendezvous, and that was the last anybody in our family ever saw of him. He just vanished. His disappearance was a real mystery to all the Fitzgeralds and it was talked about for long afterwards. Many theories were put forward, one of my uncle Dick's being that it had something to do with under cover work for the army. All my Uncle Dicks efforts to find him were in vain. I remember Johnny as a very pleasant lad who always had a smile on his face and a bag of sweets for us kids. He also disappeared one day never to be heard of again, Winnie also dropped out of our lives, but turned up again many years later and all this time she had been living in the same town of Middleton as us. I would love to know what terrible thing had happened to cause this break up of Uncle Dick's family, but I couldn't ask Winnie because she seemed to be very bitter about whatever had happened.

Some of my best memories of those times are about the yearly Whit walks, when our Mams would scrub us clean, wash our hair with carbolic soap and dress us in our best clothes and we would walk in procession through the streets of Manchester carrying large holy banners and walking behind the St Malachi's Ceilidh band. Anybody who saw these angelic little children dressed up in their best clothes, their hands and faces scrubbed clean, would never have guessed what streetwise little terrors most of them were! I never found out where the walks ended because as we were passing the Angel Inn on Oldham Road the Fitzgeralds and the Williams always left the procession and retired for some liquid refreshment. The reason that was given for this was that the poor little children's legs were tired and would never walk the full course, so we might as well stop here and rest. The innkeeper always let us kids in as long as we behaved and didn't drink any alcohol. I was glad because my little legs were incapable of walking any number of miles anyway, and the local imbibers would always give us pennies after they had a few pints.

Other abiding memories are of the rag and bone man and the knife and scissor sharpener. The rag and bone man used to come round once a week with his pony and cart which was piled high with old rags. I suppose that everything was being recycled then to help the war effort. We knew he was coming because we could hear his bugle when he was still a few streets away. No money was ever used, for any old clothes that we could give him he would give my mum a donkey stone for stoning the front door step, or we kids would get a balloon tied on a stick. Not that my Mam had many old clothes to give away. It always puzzled me how old rags could help the war effort. Usually any old clothes were cut up into strips about six inches long and woven into sackcloth to make rugs and old woollen jumpers were unravelled for knitting wool. The knife and scissor sharpener would come with his grindstone on a hand cart. It was worked by a treadle and it was fascinating for us kids to watch the sparks flying and see how expertly he handled it. Once I remember a man came with a home-made cart. It had a cage covered with a cloth and a handwritten sign proclaiming, 'Come and see the biggest Rat in the world; only 1d to view it'. Most of the kids dashed home to get a penny from their Mams. My Mam gave me a penny, then we all gathered around it. When the man had enough pennies, he pulled the cloth off the cage with a flourish; we had all been agog with excitement expecting some massive, vicious snarling beast, but it was just an ordinary rat cowering in the corner of the cage. One of the bigger kids looked at it with disdain all over his face, and shouted, "That's not the biggest rat in the world. I saw a bigger dead rat in the canal. I want me money back. Come on you, gimme me money back!" The man quickly covered the rat's cage and snarled, "Don't be so bloody cheeky yer little monkey, shut it or I'll give yer a clout across yer ear'ole." The kid replied: "I'm gonna tell me Dad" and he ran off and the last we saw of the man he was making a hasty retreat up the road and round the corner as quickly as he could push his cart.

There was also a man who went round the streets pushing a cart that had a barrel organ on it. He would stop in our street and turn a handle and the music would come floating down the street. There was no social security in those days and if you didn't work then you didn't eat. People would turn their hands to anything to make a few pennies. There was the pikelet man, who came round selling crumpets (they were called pikelets in the olden times) and also muffins and ginger cake. Mam never bought any from him, she said you don't know where he got them from or how old they were. The milkman didn't deliver the milk in bottles like he does now, on his cart he had some milk churns and he would pour a measure of milk into your jug. I'm not sure if my memory is playing tricks, but I seem to remember that in the district where mostly Irish people lived he also delivered bottles of Guinness.

One man who lived near us would go round the pubs and his speciality was swallowing needles and eating electric light bulbs. My Dad told me about him, his name was Mr Keogh. He used to live just up the road from us but he wasn't alive anymore. I wonder why? I would have liked to have seen him perform! Another man would go around the streets singing for pennies. Often my Dad would give me a penny for him and I had to tell him would he please go into the next street because my Dad was trying to sleep. And then there were the ice cream men. There were many Italians who lived in nearby Miles Platting and Ancoats who made delicious ice cream. They would come round with their ice cream carts, many of which were push carts, not motor or pony driven. I will always remember 'Pandolfo's Ice-cream' – my Mam could always find some coppers for us to have an ice cream.

There was a piece of waste ground known locally as the Albert Memorial Croft, just off Queens Road, and every summer during the 'Wakes' there would be a fairground there.

The 'Wakes' was the annual summer holiday in the Lancashire cotton towns and there was always a fair, so wakes and fair came to mean the same thing. It had all kinds of rides and stalls all designed to part the kids from their pennies. There were the roundabouts and the unforgettable 'Big Boats' (a swing that had a couple of barge-sized boats that held about fifteen to twenty people in each). The waltzers were a thrilling ride for us kids. They would spin us round, first one way then the other way, then up and down, and it would send us dizzy. Then there were the coconut shies, where I am sure the coconuts were glued to the stands and impossible to knock off with the light wooden balls. There were also boxing booths where the local hard men would go and get their heads battered by the professional pugilists, who always managed to look bored as they were punching the living daylights out of the local toughs. Then there were the black pea soup and black puddings and mustard. The pennies that I had been saving up for months went in just half an hour, but I thought it was worth it.

Then, of course, what kid of those times could forget 'Children's Hour' or 'Ramsbottom and Enoch' on the wireless. They were called wirelesses because they ran off batteries. We had two batteries for our wireless, one in use and one at the hardware shop on Queens Road being charged. We would take the battery to be changed for a fully-charged one every week, which only cost a penny or two. Posh people had radios that were plugged into the electric mains, but our wireless was just as good.

Every Mancunian over a certain age will have fond memories of Belle Vue, known as the Showground of the North. The name Belle Vue was synonymous with entertainment, variety, thrills, fun and laughter. It was a magical playground for people of all ages. There was dancing to the orchestra in the ballroom for the old people, and then there was the funfair, which included the 'Bobs', the highest rollercoaster in the world at the time, called the caterpillar, a scenic railway, water chute and many other thrilling rides. There was boxing and wrestling in the King's Hall, and the speedway. I have not even mentioned the zoo yet, with its vast array of exotic animals and elephant rides for the kids. I was always fascinated by the lion pacing backwards and forwards in its cage for what must have been hours. Many years later, when thinking about it, I realised that the poor lion was being driven mad by being confined in such a small space when its natural habitat was the wide open African spaces. There were many other shows, exhibitions and side shows, too many to mention, suffice to say that a day out to Belle Vue was an occasion never to be forgotten. To us kids the yearly visit to the circus at Christmas time was the highlight of the year. Also at Christmas time there was the Pantomime at Queens Park Hippodrome. So, growing up in the Manchester of the 1940s did have its attractions. In fact, it may seem strange but I think that in many ways, apart from the horrors of the bombing, we kids of wartime Britain had a better childhood than today's kids.

I remember going to Maine Road to watch Manchester City with our Jimmy, Kevin Collins and some other local lads. Poor as we were we could always get in the football ground. It was only a penny or two for us kids to get in, plus a penny each for bus fare on the number 53 bus. I thought that Frank Swift, City's goalie, was the best goalie in the world and we always tried to get a position behind Frank's goal. We only went fortnightly because Manchester United were using City's ground too because their own ground had been bombed, and because none of us were United fans. I must have been all of six years old and our Jimmy and his pals were two years older; it would be unthinkable to allow such young kids to make their way across town unaccompanied by an adult nowadays.

Maybe the Government of the time had ordered all this to keep the people's morale up. We seemed to have much more freedom than today's kids. We could go outside and play all day long, then come home for our tea, have a bath and go to bed and sleep the sleep of the innocent. Our parents never had to worry about us being murdered or kidnapped like parents do today, as long as we came home before it went dark all was right in our world. Maybe all the murderers and weirdos had been called up into the forces and were away fighting the war. We didn't have phones so we could constantly phone home to let Mam know we were alright, and if we listen to today's health and safety experts, it's a wonder we survived beyond our fifth birthdays. We played with and sucked lead soldiers, other toys were painted with lead-based paints, and they were chewed too. Some kids had little glass phials containing what they called 'Quick Silver', of which they would pour a bit onto their palms and roll it about to show us. I now realise it was mercury, a very strong poison. I have no idea where they got them from. You must remember that these were not normal times, we were at war and people had access to many dangerous substances through working in munitions factories. It's rather frightening to think of it now.

Another of the things that is different now from those far off days is the neighbourliness. People always had time to chat in the street or over the garden fence, and people looked out for each other, though sometimes that could be a bad thing. For example, one day a man came looking for John Griffiths, a well-known local man who lived in our street. Everybody denied knowing him because that man could have been a policeman, detective or debt collector, or even a gangster. He finally got the truth from a little kid who didn't know better and turned out to be a distant relative from some foreign country who came over to help in the war.

We could have many a very enjoyable Saturday wandering around an extremely interesting area of Manchester between Tib Street, with its many interesting shops, and Smithfield Market all the way to Shude Hill, where the barrow boys sold all kinds of things. As well as the usual vegetables, they also sold live chicks, rabbits, ferrets, puppies, kittens, pigeons etc. There were also some second hand book stalls; in fact, they were the forerunners of today's car boot sales. I remember once seeing a strongman. He was not very big and he was stripped to the waist and had a hard sinewy physique. He had several iron bars and horseshoes and would pass his hat round for donations before he would do his strongman act, bending the bars round his neck or his knee and the horseshoes into S shapes. He bent one bar by smashing it down across his forearm, which I thought was amazing.

One day, about a year later, I was walking home from Barney's house. There was a wooden fence about seven foot high, or so it seemed to me. I had always walked round it before, but this time, for some incomprehensible reason, I decided to climb over it instead. A likely explanation is that I was in my commando mode, imagining that I was on a raid in Nazi Germany. I was undaunted by the fact that there was barbed wire along the top of the fence. Kids sometimes do daft things – that wouldn't stop a commando would it? So anyway, I jumped up as high as I could to get a hand hold near the top of the fence, then I swung around to get a hold with my other hand. I peered over the top to make sure there was no enemy in sight, then I scrabbled around with my feet until I found a foothold. As I was trying to swing my leg over the fence I impaled it on a nail that was sticking out of the wood. I shouted out in pain, "OOWW!" I lost my balance and fell over head first. As I was falling I grabbed the barbed wire and impaled my hand on the barbs too. I continued to fall and the nail and barbs were ripped out, and my trousers were ripped in pieces as well. I landed awkwardly on my left hand and my arm broke with an audible crack, the pain from my leg and hand being forgotten because of the greater pain from my broken arm.

There was nobody about as I lay there for a few moments on the ground crying and writhing in pain. Eventually I got to my feet and made for home holding my broken arm and crying and shouting at the top of my voice "MAAM, I've torn my trousers! WAAAH, I've hurt my arm, MAAM. I've torn my trousers and hurt my arm. I'm sorry MAAM, WAAAH." I knew Mam would find it hard to replace my trousers because clothes were rationed. I must have been making a lot of noise because Mrs Atherton, Ken's mam, came out to see and said, "What on earth have you done Kevin dear?" She saw that I was covered in blood and in considerable pain, so she scooped me up and carried me home. This is just one of the many shocks that I gave my long suffering mam. An ambulance was duly called and I was carted off to Ancoats hospital. I was already known to the nurses there from past escapades. Only a few days before I was taken to this hospital and had stitches put into my head where it had been accidentally split open with a cricket bat by a kid from our street. A pretty nurse greeted me. "Hello Kevin, have you come to see me again?" I couldn't remember the nurse's name, but I knew that after my mum I loved her next and I wanted to marry her when I grew up. I was given chloroform, my arm was set and put in plaster and my wounds were dressed. I had to stay in hospital overnight. I'm sure that I didn't sleep a wink that night, but what seemed like ten minutes later Mam and Auntie Ruth had come to take me home. When Mam asked me why I was climbing over the fence when I could have easily walked round it, I told her that I was a commando looking for Nazis to kill. Mam and Auntie Ruth looked at each other and shook their heads in puzzlement. It was a boy thing so I didn't really expect them to understand. They told me that everyone was talking about me and I had become quite a local celebrity. Mam said, "Don't worry about the trousers Kevin, Auntie Ruth will get some for you."

Next day, when mam wasn't looking, I went out to play football with the lads and bask in their admiration and show off my plaster of paris arm cast. I bragged that it was broken in twenty places and the doctors had never seen a broken arm as bad as mine, and they said that I was the bravest boy that they had ever seen in all the world!

Were we a product of the hard times that we were living in or were we made of sterner stuff than today's kids? I don't know the answer to that, but I am glad that my kids didn't have to grow up in wartime.

Sometimes we saw American soldiers, who always seemed so smartly dressed with lots of money. They were laid back and easy going and if we asked them nicely, "Got any gum chum?" they would give us some chewing gum, and if we were lucky, some chocolate. One day I approached one of the Yanks and asked for some gum. He had no chewing gum but gave me a bar of chocolate instead. He then asked me if I had a big sister. I said, "Yes."

"How old is she?

"Nineteen."

"What's her name?"

"Betty."

"Has she got a boy friend?"

"No."

"I'll give you some more chocolate if you ask her to meet me?"

"Alright, I will, if you give me the chocolate first."

He gave me two more bars of chocolate on the strength of my fictitious sister Betty. We were certainly streetwise little urchins. Thinking, back the poor lads must have been homesick and missing their wives and girlfriends back home.

Notwithstanding the hard times and the wartime rationing, we were happy kids, I presume because we didn't know any different and couldn't remember a time when food, sweets and toys were plentiful.

Living a few streets away was a man who couldn't hear or talk. His name was Mr Arthur Thresh. Whenever Barney and I saw him we would point at our wrists, meaning "What time is it?" and he would hold up the number of fingers to indicate the time. I thought it must be terrible to be unable to hear or speak like that. Little did I know there were whole communities of people like that and that one day I would be involved with them? I would even marry a girl who couldn't hear or speak.

Another time, Mam said, "Kevin, I'm going to the shops. I don't know how long I'll be. Will you look after the fire for me and don't let it go out? I want lots of hot water for Dad's bath tonight. I can't ask Jimmy, I don't know where he is. He's out playing with his friends Kevin Collins and Roy Gill. I'm asking you because you are the sensible one anyway." I didn't know that I was the sensible one, and I was surprised that Mam thought I was, but I knew that Mam may have to queue a long time for bread, and I always tried to be positive and helpful even at that age, so I said, "Alright Mam, don't worry, I'll look after it." So Mam went off to the shops and I went out to play, and promptly forgot all about the fire.

Some time later I suddenly remembered, "Ohh, bloody 'ell, the fire!" I dashed home, but the fire was out. I tried blowing on it as I had seen Mam do; no good, it didn't work. I tried putting some newspaper and sticks and coal on, then blowing it; again no good. I sat down and pondered the problem. What to do? I mustn't let Mam down, I'd promised her I would look after the fire. What to do? Then I had a bright idea. Dad had a bottle of paraffin in his tool cupboard. I'd been told by Dad never to mess about in his tool cupboard, but this was an emergency, so I went and got it. I poured some into a cup and with fingers crossed threw it on the dead fire. At first nothing happened, then some thin wisps of white smoke began to curl up the chimney. I bent over to blow it when it suddenly ignited with a whoosh. When Mam came home I was sitting there with a blackened face, no eyebrows, my nose was scorched red and the hair at the front of my head all burnt and frizzy, but I was proud of the fact that the fire was blazing away merrily, and there would be lots of hot water for Dad's bath that night. There were no health and safety rules in those days.

Sometime after this, when I was six or seven years old, I came across our Pat crying. "What's the matter our Pat, why are you crying?" She said, "That John Mills hit me." John Mills is not his name, I will call him that because I can't remember his real name. He was about eight years old, but that didn't stop me. "Right! That's it," I said, "Nobody hits my sister." I went looking for John Mills and found him playing with some other kids. "Hey you, you hit my sister, now I'm gonna bash you." He just laughed and Ken, who was there, said, "Kev, you can't bash John, he's too big, he's the cock of the street." "Come on then," I said to John, and we squared up to each other. The very first punch, I hit him with a roundhouse right and caught him right on his nose, which started to bleed, and he began to cry. "I'm gonna tell me mam," he squealed and ran off home. I remember my hand hurt, it felt like I had broken something, but I said nothing and after a day or so the pain stopped. I took our Pat home and a few minutes later John and his mam knocked on the door. When my mam opened the door John's mam shouted at my mam something like, "Are you going to keep that hooligan under control, look what he has done to my poor John." She was holding John by the scruff of his neck and pointing at his nose with her other hand. John was standing there blubbering with blood coming from his nose, My mam said, "Do you want me to stop the bleeding from his nose, or are you going to be a proper mam and do it yourself. Anyway, he's twice my Kevin's size, and you can tell him to stop hitting little girls, now sod off" and she closed the door. Poor Mam and Dad, how we must have tried their patience.

I can remember our Jimmy coming home once covered in paint. He and his pals had gone into the paint stores in one of the nearby building sites, which must have tested Mam and Dad's patience to its limit. I cannot remember ever being punished by Mam or Dad and I think that Jimmy, Patricia and I were very lucky to have such kind parents, not that our little Pat ever did anything to be punished for.

PART TWO

I become deaf

ONE OF MY MOST poignant memories is of a day sometime around the same period. I know that I had passed my sixth birthday, but I had not yet reached my seventh birthday. After school this particular day Barney and I decided not to go home straightaway as we had promised our mams. We thought that we would explore an interesting-looking place down by the river. The River Irk was a foul-smelling river and it was in full spate from all the recent rain. It wasn't raining this particular day, but there was a kind of wet mist that hung in the air and seemed to penetrate right through your clothes and leave them soaking wet. Everything was dank and miserable, but it didn't dampen our spirits.

As we played on the river bank we were imagining Germans behind every bush. I shouted to Barney, "I've just killed hundreds of Jerries Barney, I got 'em with my tommy gun." Barney shouted back, "I've shot down ten German aeroplanes with my tommy gun, rat tat tat tat, rat tat tat." Just then I slipped on the wet and muddy river bank and slid down the slope on my bum and went into the river. I went under the filthy water and came up choking and gasping for air some yards downstream. I was flailing my arms about in a panic as I was being swept away in the torrent, and I just managed to grab hold of some long grass that was growing at the water's edge and hanging over the banks. Barney came cautiously down to help me out, but he was too small to reach me. "Hang on Kev, I'll go and get help," screamed Barney.

It seemed that he had been gone for ages and the water was freezing cold, my teeth were chattering and I was shivering uncontrollably. I was afraid to try pulling myself out by the grass as it felt like I would quite easily pull it out of the soil. I realised that I couldn't hold on much longer. Then, just as my hold was about to give out, a hand grabbed me by the back of my coat and pulled me out. I never found out the name of the man who pulled me out of the river and I never had the chance to thank him because at that moment he was a very angry man, he was shouting at us, "Yer stupid little idjits, what the effing 'ell d'yer fink yer doin', hey! Get away from 'ere afore I give yer the back of me 'and across yer effin' ear'oles. It's too effing dangerous for kids to play 'ere. Go on, scram, eff off home with you'se." Those were not his actual words, he was using some very strong Anglo Saxon words, a lot worse than these, and my word checker won't let me use the actual words. He was staggering about a bit and he smelled of beer, but we understood what he meant, so we scurried off home before I froze. He must have been a typical rough and ready Mancunian who didn't like to show that he really had a heart of gold because he thought that people would think he was soft.

I told Barney, "I'm off 'ome now Barney, 'cos I'm cold and my head is hurting, and I'll see you in the morning, bye." On the way home my headache was getting worse, and by the time I was at my door the pain was intense, it felt like it was splitting open and I was shaking uncontrollably. I couldn't focus on the door and I had just enough strength to get the key from the string around my neck and somehow manage to find the keyhole and open the door. I don't know why I didn't just knock on the door. I went in and collapsed in front of Jimmy and Pat and Kevin Collins, one of our Jimmy's friends, who were sitting around the wireless listening to 'Children's Hour'. They must have been shocked to see me stagger in and collapse. Being two years older than me, our Jimmy had his own circle of friends and Kevin Collins, who lived up the road at Kingsley Crescent, was his best friend. Kevin had no Mam so our Mam treated him like another son, and he was always at our house.

I don't know how long I was comatose but it must have been a long time, a few days at least because I felt very weak when I next opened my eyes. I thought, 'Oh good, my headache has gone', then I thought it all seemed so strangely different. I lay there staring at the ceiling wondering what it was that made everything seem so different, but I couldn't put my finger on it. I just lay there thinking that it was all very quiet, usually in our house there was always some noise, someone was always talking, arguing or singing and there was always the sound of kids playing in the street or the wireless blaring away. Now there was just this peculiar silence; it felt as if I was the only person in the world. After a while Mam came into the room, saw that I was awake and came over and started talking to me. But she was just moving her mouth, no sound was coming from her! I said, "What's the matter Mam, why are you doing that? Can't you speak?" Then I realised that no sound was coming from my mouth either. I didn't understand it, what was going on? Why was everything different, as if I was another person in a different world. It was some time before I realised that I was deaf and I couldn't hear a thing, that was why everything seemed so strange. A few weeks later, when I had become used to being deaf, Mam told me that it was thanks to our Dr Duguid that I was still alive. He had spent hours at my bedside, and had somehow managed to get drugs that were in short supply because of the war and were meant only for the soldiers. Mam said that Dr Duguid was a good man; he was a very clever doctor and could have been very rich if he had chosen to practise in one of the posh areas. Instead, he chose to work in Collyhurst amongst the poor. There was no NHS then, you had to pay the doctor for any treatment, but Mam said that Dr Duguid never charged a penny. Doctors are not like that nowadays are they?

It was hard for Mam and me to communicate at first, Mam had to turn my face towards her so that I could see her mouth, then she would speak to me using exaggerated mouth movements. The Doctor had told my Mam and Dad that they must do that when communicating with me from now on. It was a slow process, but we got there in the end, and with practise we became quite fast at communicating that way. Some of my friends from the street and school were allowed in to visit me. They were all standing and sitting round the bed, all chattering away, and I didn't have a clue what they were talking about, but nevertheless I was very pleased to see them again. They had brought me some comics, the 'Dandy' and 'Beano'. My Dad had made me a wooden fort and Mam had got me some lead soldiers and we had some fun playing with them, but never again would I be able to listen to the wireless. Even at that early age I had loved listening to Gracie Fields, Richard Tauber, and George Formby etc.

It was some weeks before I was allowed out of bed. Mam, Dad, Jimmy and Pat and some friends all came for the big day when I would be allowed out of bed. On first putting my feet on the floor, it felt really weird. They felt very soft and puffy and when taking my first step I would have fallen over if my Dad and Jimmy had not caught me. It was like trying to walk on pillows. I was very weak and I had to learn to walk all over again. This time I would also have to learn to be more aware of my surroundings. I found out that when I could hear I took a lot of what was happening behind me for granted because I could more or less hear what was going on behind, but when I couldn't hear it was different because people would suddenly appear from behind me into my line of vision with no warning at all. It was very disconcerting and I found myself continually turning my head around to see behind me. It took me a long time to get accustomed to not knowing what was happening behind me. At first it was a scary experience to go out to play without our Jimmy or Pat as the other kids would speak to me and I didn't know what they were saying. Everybody was being nice to me and I would just stand there looking at them feeling stupid. It was really making me realise how important my hearing and the ability to communicate was. We don't understand just how important that ability is until we lose it.

It was quite an adventure to go out on a foggy day when visibility was low. I couldn't do it alone, especially if it was a peasouper, I had to have someone with me to hold my hand. It was almost as if I was blind as well as deaf, and my balance was all out of kilter. I adopted a strange way of walking, with one side of my body in advance of the other, rather like a dog when it sidles along. There was a smidgeon of hearing still in my right ear and I was compensating for the complete loss of hearing in my left ear. When people said something to me I would crane my head forward with my right ear advanced. I found that my balance was not as good as before I became deaf and I had difficulty walking in a straight line.

Was the fall into the murky River Irk the cause of my having meningitis? Would I have caught meningitis anyway? Was my immune system weakened by the fall into the river? Or was it weakened by the wartime diet and lack of sleep because of the air raids? Was the meningitis germ already incubating inside me? I don't know the answer to these questions, I never asked. I just accepted the fact that I couldn't hear anymore. I was too young to understand the affect that being deaf would have on my life; the bullying, the bigotry, the barriers, the stigma that was attached to being deaf was beyond my understanding.

Now, with the acumen of age, I know how to handle the people who think that they can use my deafness to their advantage, and there have been many. I firmly believe that deaf people can have very useful, fruitful and happy lives if they are given a good education and learn to read and write the Queen's English. They can become more autonomous and rely less on interpreters and social workers. Deafness is only a problem because of communication difficulties. They are deaf, there is nothing wrong with their eyes, and if deaf people could read and write they could always use a pen and paper if they got stuck, and there would be far more information available to them via books, newspapers, computers etc.

Some people have intolerable attitudes towards deaf people, and the so-called educated people are the worst. Many of them just pay lip service to such things as Deaf Awareness, Equal Opportunities and social inclusion and it may all be caused by an inability to communicate between the deaf and hearing people. I have been giving this phenomenon a lot of thought lately and I think that it may be an innate instinct for the preservation of the species. This same phenomenon can be observed in the animal world, any animal that is different or any baby animals born with defects are killed or got rid of some other way. Nevertheless, it is still our world. It may not be fair, but it can still be good and we must make the best of it. I have devised a system of dealing with such negative people. It may not work for everyone, but it works for me. In my mind I will try, whenever possible, to see and believe that I am as good as, if not a better person than, these people. I make it an unfailing rule to always choke off and completely block off every negative thought these people try to put into my mind. The moment it begins to take form in my mind, wipe it out, destroy it and replace it with something positive. This is not difficult to do, it takes a determined effort and it may be awkward at first, but it gets easier with practice.

As long as a deaf person or any other handicapped person lives, they will encounter barriers, problems and obstacles caused by bigots. Our only option is how we will face and deal with these obstacles, not whether or not they will exist. Choose to face them as a challenge, not a burden, and resolve to beat them, not be beaten by them.

I will quote some words from Victor Hugo, which I have found to be very true:

What matter deafness of the ear when the mind hears,
The one true deafness, the incurable deafness,
is deafness of the mind.

As I recovered and got stronger my Mam took me to see the specialists at Manchester University. Professor Ewing and his wife were the top specialists in deafness at that time and they now have a wing of the university named after them. I remember that Mrs Ewing tested my hearing. She had a metal thing with two prongs that she would bang on the table, then hold close to my ear. "Can you hear that?" "No." Then she did the same with my other ear with the same result. Next she gave me some tests to do, like putting round blocks into round holes and square blocks into square holes and so on. I remember thinking, 'How is this going to bring my hearing back?' Then she put two tubes up my nostrils. They were attached to a rubber ball, which she then proceeded to squeeze and send gusts of air up my nose. I thought she was going to blow my head off. She told my Mam that it would clear my sinuses and maybe bring back my hearing. She also told my Mam that a simple thing like a bang on my head or some other kind of shock could bring my hearing back. When my Mam pointed out to her that I had a nerve deafness caused by meningitis and not blocked sinuses she just said "Oh" and made an appointment for us to see her again at a future date. Maybe she just didn't want to upset my Mam any more than she already was and was saying what she thought my Mam wanted to hear. I have had many knocks and bangs on my head since those days, but sadly I am still deaf.

At our next visit to Professor Ewing she commented on our surname, Fitzgerald, and asked my Mam if we were Catholics. My Mam answered her, "Yes, we are." Professor Ewing then advised my Mam that the best course of action would be to send me to St John's School for the Deaf and Dumb [sic] at

Boston Spa in Yorkshire, as it was the only school for Catholic deaf children in Britain. Of course, I didn't know at the time what was being said by Professor Ewing and my Mam. Mam told me about it later.

Then we were sent to a place in Hardman Street, which was off Deansgate in Manchester, so that I could be fitted with one of the most modern super duper hearing aids of the time. The hearing aids of the 1940s were not like the tiny behind the ear hearing aids of today. This one was a massive contraption, with two big round Bakelite earpieces connected by a metal band that went over my head. Plastic had yet to be invented. The battery was in a leather case and must have weighed about five pounds. It certainly felt as if it did! It was worn on my left side by a leather strap that went around my neck, and the receiver was slightly smaller and was in a leather case to be worn on my right side by another leather strap that went around my neck from the other side. The connecting wires from the receiver to the earpieces and from the battery to the receiver went up and across the front of my body and got in the way of my arms, so I had to be careful how I moved them. I felt weighed down with it and I had to wear it on the way home. I felt very self conscious and that people were staring at me. It was awful. I couldn't see how I could play football or run about with it on and I couldn't hear anything clearly with it anyway. I certainly couldn't recognise any of the words that people were saying, only strange noises that tended to confuse me. A car would be right on top of me before I could hear it. Around my neck I also had to carry my gas mask in a cardboard box. It was all too much for a little kid to carry around all day, so we all agreed that it was best to put it in a drawer and never be seen again.

Someone told Mam about this place in Wales where the water had miraculous properties, so Mam took me on a coach from the bus station in Moseley Street in Manchester to St. Winifred's Well in North Wales to get some Holy water to pour down my ears. We also took a large lemonade bottle to fill up at the holy spring and bring home with us so we could put some in my ears every night before bed, and Jimmy and Patricia had to say a prayer for me. Mam was leaving nothing to chance and she would do whatever she could to help me to hear again. She had also bought a scapula that contained a fraction of the Holy Saints' bone. This I was to wear around my neck and I had to hold it in my hands while Mam, Jimmy, Patricia and me said Hail Mary and Our Father every night. All this was supposed to make me hear again.

Going to Lourdes was not possible because of the war, but my Mam promised that when the war was over she would take me there and make me better. By the time the war was over I think she had realised that it was a false hope and had given up. She had come to terms with the realisation that there was nothing that would bring my hearing back again. My Mam was more worried about my deafness than I was; perhaps she knew better than me what the future as a deaf person had in store. I was too young to really understand how precious your sense of hearing is and what a big loss it was. It must have been breaking my Mam's heart to see me so helpless in the hearing world. I don't say much about my Dad, but as I grew up I realised that my Dad was heartbroken about my deafness too, he just wasn't good at showing his emotions, but I know he loved us very much too because I had learned to read facial expressions and body language by then, so even though he never said much, I knew. My Mam was very protective of me and so were my Brother Jimmy and even our little Patricia. I did find it suffocating sometimes and I think that Auntie Ruth could see that because I often caught her telling my Mam to "Leave him alone, let him fight his own battles, he is quite capable of looking after himself."

One day my Mam told me that I had to go away to a special school where they would teach me to hear again, so in September 1942, when I was seven years old, she packed a little suitcase with spare stockings, shirts, etc. and took me to the Exchange railway station in Manchester. It was the first time that I had seen a train close up; it was a massive scary monster belching smoke and steam that made the ground rumble and sent vibrations up my legs. My first train ride was a very exciting experience and I had my head out of the window most of the time. My Mam kept telling me to get my head in and sit down, but I was too excited to sit still. The train took us to Leeds, where we walked out of the station. We were supposed to get a bus at Vicar Lane that would take us to Boston Spa, which was about fourteen miles away, but as we walked out of the station my Mam began to cry and she kept hugging me, and to see my Mam crying like that made me cry too, so we sat down on a bench outside the station and hugged and cried together. People passing by must have wondered what was going on because we were getting some curious looks from the passers by. Suddenly my Mam looked at me, she turned my head so that I could see her mouth and she said, "I'm not doing it, we are going home Kevin, come on," I said, "Alright Mam, that's a good idea!" So we quickly dried our eyes and went back into the station and caught the next train home.

At St Malachi's the teacher was surprised to see me walk into the classroom the next morning. The headmaster, Mr Power, was informed and he sent for my Mam. When she arrived at the school I too was sent to Mr Power's office. She was giving him a piece of her mind and wagging her finger in his face. After a few minutes arguing my Mam took hold of my hand and we went home. Next day Mam took me again to the railway station, but this time she was not taking me to Leeds. No, this time we got a train to Blackpool, no Jimmy, no Patricia, just me and Mam. It was the first time that I had seen the sea and I was very impressed to see how big it was. It was easy for me to imagine sharks and other sea monsters lurking in the depths. We had brought some sandwiches so we sat on a bench on the promenade and ate them. I realised later, when thinking about that day, that Mam was spending as much time as she could with me before I was sent away. A few days later one of the teachers from St Malachi's came to our house to tell mam that I would be allowed back in the school until something was sorted out.

This is the time of my life when I first noticed a change in some people's attitude towards me. They seemed to shy away from talking to me. Even Barney wasn't the same; it was almost as if I was being shunned. It would be many years in the future when I would finally understand that they were simply afraid that I wouldn't understand them, and that could lead to some embarrassing situations, but at the time I was very upset and puzzled by this change in people's behaviour. I was still me, I was still Little Fitzy, wasn't I? Also, this is the time that I was perfecting my lip-reading ability. The ability to lip-read and understand body language and facial expressions happens naturally if you were hearing before becoming deaf; if you are born deaf then you have a much more difficult time of it.

All through my schooldays and early working life I could manage with no difficulty as long as I was communicating with just one person. If any more people joined in, the conversation then became much more difficult for me to follow. When I was in the building trade I always tried not to get embroiled in any arguments, but sometimes arguments are forced on you and there is no escaping them. At first I was considered to be not a full shilling, and when I won an argument the other person looked upon it as an affront to his dignity and would turn his head away and continue talking to the others and I wouldn't know what he said, so I tried to avoid arguments and discussions. I suppose that they didn't have an easy life. The working man in those days didn't have the same level of protection against greedy employers that they have today and most of them were not very clever and were exploited by some unscrupulous employers, so they needed someone who they could focus their resentments on, and they thought that being deaf I was an easy target. That was a mistake on their part.

I remember well one winter after it had been snowing and the lads on the site were larking about throwing snowballs. Big Jock was the gaffer (foreman) on this job. Big Jock was a legend, nobody messed with big Jock, do you hear me! Nobody messed with Big Jock, Right! Big Jock was as hard as nails. He used to be in the Royal Marines during the war and he was throwing snowballs too, but nobody was throwing snowballs back at big Jock. Being deaf I had not heard about big Jock's reputation as a hard man. I caught him with a snowball on the side of his head and snow went down inside his shirt. I laughed and shouted "Gotcha". He went red with anger, roaring, "You little bastard" and ran over to me and grabbed hold of my head and put me in a head lock. I thought that he was still larking about so I gave as good as I got, then it began to get serious because he was rubbing my nose on his belt buckle and it was hurting and cutting it. I asked him to stop and he wouldn't. I asked him to stop again and again he wouldn't stop, so I reached up behind his back and over his head and stuck two fingers up his nose and yanked him off me. He gave a yelp and went off some way holding his nose which was bleeding at the sides where the skin was torn. All the others gathered around him. "Are you alright Jock?" they were saying as they looked at me and gave me dirty looks. I thought, "What a bunch of creeps." I had read somewhere that Irwin Rommel had said that the British were a nation of lions led by donkeys. Well this lot were certainly not lions; they were more like bunny rabbits.

Because of my deafness I hadn't heard that I wasn't supposed to mess with big Jock. All I knew was that he was messing with me, and I wasn't having that. I wonder if I could have heard like the rest of them would I have acted like them too? I wouldn't like to think that I would. I know that I hadn't heard of the legend of big Jock, so it wasn't playing tricks with my mind. I just went ahead and sorted out the problem. It never even entered my mind that Big Jock was someone to be scared of.

I was expecting trouble after that and I was ready for it. At this time of my life I was a keen weightlifter, and I also wrestled and boxed at the YMCA, so when Big Jock and I were messing about that day I could feel that his body was soft and he wasn't in the same condition he must have been in his Royal Marine days. Nothing happened, however. Maybe they thought that being deaf I was not normal, perhaps even slightly mad, so it was better to leave me alone. The funny thing about that episode is that Big Jock became a great friend of mine and always asked the office if he could have me on his jobs. He ended up always talking about the incident and he would say, "Do you remember when you nearly pulled my nose off Kev" as if it was a fond memory. My lip-reading ability let me know what people were really like because they thought that I couldn't understand what they were saying and they thought that they could talk about me as if I wasn't there. They would sometimes blame me for things that I hadn't done (I told him, but he didn't hear me).

When I was working with people like that I would sometimes take a delight in making them look stupid and rubbing their noses in it, which was very easy to do when the person's ego was involved. For many years I had been brainwashed to believe that deaf people were inferior to hearing people. Now, working with these people made me realise that was not true at all, far from it. For instance, sometimes at dinner one or other of them may start doing the crossword in the newspaper, the Daily Mirror or the Sun, not the hard ones. If he got stuck he would ask the others to help him and never ask me as it was assumed that I was not clever enough to know. When they gave up and put the paper down, I would pick it up and nonchalantly finish it off. That would drive them wild. I wasn't supposed to be better than them, was I? I would take my chess set to work sometimes and after I had beaten one or two of them they would all gang up and play against me, giving contradicting advice and confusing each other. When I checkmated them I could see the frustration in their faces, but I would give a sardonic chuckle and walk off. I know it was not very nice of me, but it made me feel better.

Why did they always treat me as an outsider, as if I was a different sort of person, an alien? I was a born and bred Mancunian, and proud of it. It was my deafness that made me different, and maybe the way I pronounced words. Later on I joined up with a gang of lads and they were great with me. I think that I had gotten a bit of a reputation by then. I was told that the way I looked directly in their faces intimidated a lot of people. I was only trying to lip-read them, not scare them. Anyway, I had their respect and we travelled about going from one big job to another, going where the big money was. I didn't wear a hearing aid until some time in the 1980s when I got a tiny behind the ear one.

PART THREE

First impressions –
St John's Institution for
the Deaf and Dumb

BACK AT ST MALACHI'S over the next few months it became evident that I was not doing as well with my lessons as the other kids, so my Mam had to reluctantly give in and agree for me to be sent to St John's at Boston Spa. So, in September 1943, at the age of eight, exactly one year after our first attempt, my suitcase was packed again, but this time my Mam was forbidden by the authorities to take me. Instead, one of the nuns from St Malachi's took me. She was of a very stern visage and I could see that she would have none of that nonsense of wanting to go back home. Also travelling with me on that fateful journey was a little deaf girl from Salford whose name I learned was Nora. It was first time for her too and she was sobbing quietly in the corner seat, covering her face with her hands. I had a packet of biscuits that Mam had given me for the journey. I felt sorry for her, so I tapped her on her arm and offered her the biscuits. I only meant her to take one or two, but she took the whole packet. The nun looked at me approvingly and nodded her head, so I kept quiet and just sat opposite Nora and watched her scoffing my biscuits between sobs.

After an uneventful journey by train and bus we arrived at St John's Institution for the Deaf and Dumb [sic] on a bright, sunny September afternoon; this was to be my home for the next eight years. It was an imposing grey stone building located in some of the most beautiful countryside in England, and to me, "little Fitz" from the slums of Collyhurst and Miles Platting where the sparrows would cough instead of chirp, it was a magical wonderland. I had never seen so much green or so many trees in my life, and to breathe the pure clean country air was wonderful. That fresh air alone must have added an extra ten years to my life span. There were cows and horses in the fields too. These horses were not the same as the rag and bone man's horse, no! These horses were magnificent giant horses with big hairy legs. I could imagine the knights of old in shining armour riding these horses into battle and scaring the enemy sh... whoops! I mean witless (I nearly used another word there). I found out later that peas actually grew in pods and had to be shelled – I always thought they just came in tins. But worse than that, I discovered that milk came from cows udders and it was the milkman who put it in bottles, and eggs came from chickens bums. I was finding out a lot of things that city kids were unaware of; I had a lot to tell them when I next went home.

When we went up the stone steps and through the front door into the reception hall, I noticed how spick and span it all was and how shiny the wooden floors were and it all smelled very strongly of disinfectant. There were statues in the corners and holy pictures on the walls. I found out later that the boys were all given jobs to do and some of them had to polish all the wooden parquet floors every day. The Sisters clearly believed that the devil found work for idle hands. I also found out later that the Institution covered some eight acres and the farm that they also owned covered some fifty acres.

Boston Spa was a sleepy little village on the banks of the River Wharfe, which flows majestically along through a broad and beautiful valley. One mile away is the small village of Clifford and St John's Institution for the Deaf and Dumb is situated midway between the two villages. Actually, I don't think that Clifford deserves to be called a village as there were just a few houses clustered together, a small Church called St

Edward the Confessor, which seemed to be very old with a lofty tower looking out over the surrounding countryside and looked as if it dated from Norman times, one pub and, as far as I could see, there were no shops at all, at least I never noticed any on the few times I went there. So maybe we should call Clifford a hamlet, not a village. All the houses and buildings were built with white limestone blocks and looked very quaint. What a difference it was from Manchester, with its grimy brick buildings and where every road was lined with shops of every description and a pub on every corner. Even the water tasted different: Manchester's water was very soft, whereas Yorkshires water was very hard and limey. They say it is good for your bones, and it is used to make a very good pint of bitter in the brewery at nearby Tadcaster, but I wouldn't know about that until years later when I was grown up.

We were met in the entrance hall by an apparition in a long black gown that reached to the floor. Tied round her waist was what I recognised as a rosary, but it was much larger than an ordinary rosary, the beads were as big as marbles and a large crucifix hung down her leg. On her other side hung a large bunch of keys. On her head she wore a large white hat (cornette) made of some stiff material, which had a pointed front that jutted out in front of her by about twelve inches, and two big side wings. It was a scary sight to a little boy in a strange environment as she bore down on us with the crucifix swinging and the bunch of keys jangling and the side wings of her hat flapping like a swan's wings. Hitler's bombs had failed to scare me, but this was different. I'm sure she would have scared Flash Gordon or Hopalong Cassidy, maybe even Tarzan himself. She seemed so strange and threatening, I could not understand why any normal person would chose to dress in those medieval clothes, so I am not ashamed to admit that I gave a whimper of fear and hid behind the nun, who by then seemed quite a normal person to me. I learned later that it was Sister Lucy who had met us. She was one of the nicer sisters. Nora had been taken away by another sister while I was hiding behind the nun. The sisters were of 'The Order of the Sisters of Charity of St Vincent De Paul'.

After saying goodbye to the nun, Sister Lucy took me by the hand and led me away to a room that was full of tables and chairs. She asked, "Are you hungry?" I was very hungry, so I said "Yes". She told me to sit down at a table and went off, a few minutes later returning with a bowl of stewed apples and custard and a glass of milk. These were not dried apples but real apples and they tasted lovely. Sister Lucy went off then and left me to eat my apples and custard. I'd had nothing to eat since breakfast – Nora had eaten all my biscuits – so I soon finished it, and after looking around to make sure that nobody was watching I licked the bowl clean. My Mam had told me to always clean my plate, the German U-boats were trying to starve us into surrendering by sinking the ships bringing us food, so we mustn't waste food.

After I'd eaten I didn't know what to do, so I just sat there and examined my environs. I was in a large room with a high ceiling, there was a goldfish in a glass tank on a table in the corner and the room had the same highly polished floor that I had seen in the entrance hall and there was a row of windows that looked out onto a large playground.

As I was looking around a lady entered the room, came up to me and said, "Hello little boy, what is your name?"

"Kevin," I replied.

"Well, Kevin, I am Miss Harker. Will you come along with me to my class."

I didn't really have a choice did I? She took hold of my hand and led me away to her classroom.

There were about fifteen boys in Miss Harker's classroom. Miss Harker told the class to say hello to me and to tell me their names. Each boy came to me and made a sign with his hands and made funny sounds and movements with their mouths, and that was my introduction to sign language and the world of the deaf.

When I understood that these boys couldn't hear, just like me, I immediately felt comfortable with them. Then I found out that they couldn't even speak. I thought, "Aw, poor kids", but I needn't have felt sorry for them because there was not a bit of self pity in any of them; why should there be? They were with their peers, they were all in the same boat here.

There was a piano in Miss Harker's classroom. She would gather the boys around it with their hands on it, play a short tune, then ask the boys, "How many?" Some boys would hold up three fingers, some would hold up four. I had no idea what it was about, so I just copied the boy next to me whose name I learned was Cyril. He was fully deaf and couldn't speak, so I marvelled at how he knew the correct number of fingers to hold up, and he was always right. I learned later that we had to count the beat of the tune and Cyril could tell by feeling the vibrations.

Miss Harker would go through the methods to teach deaf children to speak that were in vogue at that time, and it was a ritual that we had to go through every morning. In order to learn to say the letter 'M', she would hold a balloon lightly to our lips so that we could feel the vibrations and get the sound right; for the letter 'P' she held a strip of paper in front of our mouths and we would say 'P', at the same time expelling air strong enough to bend the strip of paper over; for the letter 'N' she would simply pinch one side of our nostrils together so that it came out as a nasal sound 'NNNNEH'. There was a method to use for all the sounds using balloons, paper, a mirror and doctors' spatulas and other things that I can't remember. She also used her hands. Some of the profoundly deaf boys who had great difficulty trying to speak seemed to exasperate her. She would stick her fingers in their mouths and push and pull their tongues in her efforts to make them speak and she was very impatient with some of the boys. "Do it like this," she would say – 'LLLLL!' – put your tongue on the roof of your mouth, like this – 'LLLLL!' She would put her hand in the boy's mouth and push his tongue up to the roof of his mouth. Sometimes the poor boys would be squirming and gagging, their faces turning purple and eyes watering in their efforts to breathe while she was pulling and pushing on their tongues in her frustration at being unable to get them to speak properly. The one thing that teachers of deaf children need in abundance, above all other qualities, is patience, which was sadly lacking with Miss Harker.

There was nothing wrong with my speech, I already had speech before I became deaf, but I still had to go through with the speech lessons. Perhaps my voice was overly loud because I hadn't yet got control over it because of not being able to hear it, or maybe she didn't understand my Manchester accent. Some of the words I used were strange to her. I would say "Look" or "Book" and she would correct me and say I must say "Luk" and "Buk" and other strange sounding words. She didn't even know what a jam butty was, and every time I tried to explain to her what it was she would start giggling and ask me to say it again, giggling all the time. I thought it was very strange, but oddly endearing. I suppose I made a change, with my strange (to her) accent, from kids who couldn't speak at all. I only had to say something to set her off giggling again, so I tended to exaggerate my Manchester accent just to make her laugh again. However, she did teach me not to speak out of the corner of my mouth, and not to shout, and how to control the volume of my voice, and I am grateful to her for that.

She was always asking me questions about Manchester; What was it like? Was there plenty food? (I didn't think it would be prudent to tell her about my Aunty Ruth) What did people think about the bombing? About the war? What was it like in the bomb shelters? What did we do in them? Do I remember any of the songs about the war that we sang in the shelters? I said I knew one but my Dad said it was not for women to hear. She insisted that I sing it for her but my voice was not as tuneful as before I became deaf. Nevertheless, I thought I would give it a try. There were several versions of this song, so I thought it best to give her one of the tamer versions. I sang:

Oh! The fuehrer says ve are der master race!
So we'll Heil fhrrrrt!
Heil fhrrrrt!
Right in der fuehrer's face.'

She interrupted me and asked, "What is that fhrrrrt? What does it mean?"

"Well, Miss, that's why my Dad said I mustn't sing it in mixed company. You see, it's what a fart sounds like."

Miss Harker looked shocked. Then she grabbed me by my arm and marched me to the Sister Superior's office. By then I was wishing that I had chosen a song such as 'Hey Little Hen' or 'Run Rabbit Run'" Miss Harker made me repeat the song for Sister Catherine, who was the Sister Superior then. Sister Catherine was cool about it. She turned her head towards me. I guessed she was looking, but it was hard to tell because she always had very dark glasses on and I couldn't see her eyes. Then she told me to go back to my class and asked Miss Harker to stay. About ten minutes later Miss Harker came back into the classroom looking decidedly sheepish; she didn't ask me for any more songs after that.

****

Signing wasn't forbidden outside the classrooms but was discouraged in the classrooms, so contrary to what many hearing people may think, signing was not taught in Deaf Schools or institutions, but was passed down from one generation of deaf children to the next generation. Any mistakes in grammar or syntax were passed down too, which is one of the reasons for the bad grammar in BSL. The teachers did not teach the deaf children the rules of language, or if they did then the children didn't understand what they were saying, and so a type of Pidgin English in sign language had evolved over the years, maybe in the same way that the West Indian patois developed, like "Who you be? Where you is? Why you din't?" And many people living in our inner cities mangle the Queens English too, but that is their choice. The lessons that the deaf children had just didn't register. In fact, I don't think any of the deaf children learnt much at all from the teachers because most of the teachers were not very good signers and were not allowed to sign in the classroom, even if they could, because what was known as the 'Oral System' of teaching was used.

Most, if not all, of the teachers were from Manchester University and had learnt the Oral System of teaching deaf children there. The Ewings of Manchester University were staunch advocates of the Oral System. It's a pity that nobody ever thought of asking the deaf adults for their opinions on this matter. Albert Einstein defined insanity as 'Doing the same thing over and over again and expecting different results each time'. What a marvellous quote that is. The education authorities had been using the same Oral System that was turning out deaf children unable to read or write for well over 100 years, even though the deaf children had an extra year in school, leaving at the age of 16 when hearing children left at 15 years old. The deaf children were still far behind hearing children with their reading and writing skills.

Because of the Oral System, and signing being forbidden, many different systems of signing had evolved over the years. St John's at Boston Spa had a signing system that was unlike any other in use in Britain at the time. The London signing system was different to any other, as was Manchester's, Liverpool's, Wales's, and Scotland's. In fact, every deaf school or institution in Britain had a different signing system, and this was another problem the deaf had to overcome – all because signing, the language of the deaf, was not standardised and taught in deaf schools.

And so, because closed minds and red tape was winning over common sense, there was not much proper communication between teachers and children. Some of the deaf children came from families where the parents or elder siblings were deaf too, and because of this, these deaf children had been signing and communicating in a normal family environment and not treated as if deafness was an illness that separated them from "normal" children, so they had very active and confident minds and far fewer problems than the other deaf children who came from hearing families. Deaf children from deaf families often do very well at school despite the communication problems with the teachers, so they tended to be leaders and communicated what they had learnt from their families to the other deaf children. The children learnt more from them than from the teachers, except of course they didn't learn how to use English grammar, and that sad state of affairs was to blight their lives.

There were differing degrees of deafness at St John's. Most of the children were profoundly deaf and couldn't speak at all;

others, including myself, had varying degrees of hearing and could speak after a fashion. The teachers made no distinction in the children's differing needs; we were all together in the same classroom. There was a radio room where there was a big table which had about twenty sets of earphones and a microphone. Ostensibly, this was for the children who had some hearing, but this room was never used for that purpose, it was only ever used by Sister Teresa and Sister Lucy to listen to the football results every Saturday.

Most of these deaf children left school at the age of sixteen with the reading and writing ability of a hearing eight year old child, if they were lucky, because they were the clever ones. Others never learned to read or write at all. These children were DEAF, but there was nothing wrong with their eyes; all the information that they were able to gather was through their eyes.

It was clearly obvious that the oral method of teaching deaf children was a resounding failure, and it had been a failure from the first day it was introduced around 1880 when the International Congress on the Education of the Deaf met in Milan, Italy. When signing was banned in schools for the deaf, this resulted in hundreds of Deaf teachers being dismissed from their jobs and it sent Deaf Education on a downward spiral from which it has not quite recovered today. To say that the deaf have their own unique grammar is at best a ridiculous statement, and, at worst, a cover-up for the dismal failure of the teachers to teach deaf children the Queen's English. I know that when the inspectors paid a visit to St John's, the hard of hearing children were put in the front so that the teachers could show how they had taught them to speak. It is shocking that nobody in a position to do something about it had done so, and it is something that the Church and education authorities should be thoroughly ashamed of.

In America there was a Deaf/Blind lady named Helen Keller. She overcame her terrible affliction and learned to speak thanks to her dedicated teacher, Ann Sullivan. Maybe Helen was wealthy and could afford the best teacher, I don't know, but it shows what can be done. If only the UK Government would spend some money on profoundly deaf and deaf/blind children, instead of wasting money on rubbish listening to the wrong people, the so called 'experts' – and, as has been shown recently, on lining their own pockets! But I don't suppose that UK Governments want to hear about things like this. Helen Keller's story, which was made into an outstanding Hollywood film called 'The Miracle Worker', shows just what can be achieved with good teachers who have the patience to teach and the will to succeed. Helen had lost both her sight and hearing in early childhood and she had only three senses left: taste, smell and touch, and the sense of touch was the only way she could communicate. She developed that sense to a very high degree, her fingers had become very sensitive and she knew what people were saying just by touching their throats and feeling the vibrations of that person's vocal chords.

Deaf people have only lost the sense of hearing; they still have their sight, and as sign language is a visual way of communicating, then surely it stands to reason that signing is the correct way for them to learn. Before signing was banned in classrooms at the turn of the last century, deaf teachers were turning out literate deaf children and many of these deaf children went on to become professional people. I challenge any opponent of Sign Supported English to give me one single valid argument, one single piece of evidence, to show that signing that way has a bad effect on any deaf person. It is clear that the real issue is one of control. It is ridiculous to say that deaf BSL users have their own 'unique' grammar. This situation came about because hearing teachers couldn't teach deaf children the Queen's English. I cannot think of any reason why the Oral System was considered an improvement on Signing, the only reason that makes sense to me is that they wanted the deaf to be illiterate and dependent on hearing people so that the hearing people could get paid for 'helping' them, so it is all a matter of the power to control deaf people, and it is still going on today with organisations led by hearing people purporting to help the deaf while making large amounts of money by doing so.

So hearing teachers whose signing skills were very poor, or non-existent, replaced the deaf teachers and their dismal failure to teach the deaf children the English language, the language of the country they were born in, has been hidden under the guise of deaf people's 'unique' grammar. I have been told by hearing educationalists that the grammar of BSL is the deaf people's way of communicating and they cannot interfere. How on earth could these people say that? It was hearing people who interfered with the signing method of educating deaf children over 100 years ago. These are the people who have stolen the education of deaf people for so many years, and that can never be given back.

Canon Hayward, the first deaf Catholic priest in Britain, explained it best. He had been on a learning tour of America and when he came back he told us about what he had seen there. He said that there is a big difference between the British deaf and the American and Canadian deaf in their ability to understand the written word. The signs used in America and Canada are much easier for hearing people to learn because they follow the order of spoken language, and the deaf themselves have better language than the deaf in Britain because the way they sign follows the grammar of the written and spoken word and helps them to understand English much better. Nearly all deaf schools in America teach by using sign language. Gallaudet University, the only university in the world that is for deaf people, uses sign language.

I have met many deaf people from strict oral schools who now sign. They told me that their speaking was long and drawn out, like "Hel-lo, my na- me is D-a-vid", and their voices were flat, even Welsh people, who usually have very musical voices; there was no intonation at all. Hearing people would not speak to them as they found it too much trouble. They had to learn to sign and join the deaf world or they would have been isolated and lonely. Some said they left the oral schools feeling stupid and with no confidence, but later learned very quickly a lot that they had never known before because other deaf people had taught them by signing.

Some of the parents of deaf children who went to oral schools have told me how sorry they were, because when they saw how happy their children were signing to other deaf children, they realised they had been given wrong information by the oral teachers, who told them that they must try to stop their children signing as it would hinder their ability to learn to speak. These oral teachers have shown their ignorance of the problems of deafness. I agree wholeheartedly with Canon Hayward's sentiments.

We cannot blame the parents of deaf children for believing the oral propaganda – it is very comforting propaganda and, naturally, the parents want to believe it. The good of a deaf child is not in education alone, it must also include social and religious life, so the deaf must have sign language, and the best sign language for our deaf children is the one that enables them to follow the spoken and written word and thus enable them to live fuller and more rewarding lives; not a sign language that because of it's different, or 'unique', grammar cuts them off from all the information and answers to life's problems to be gleaned from books, computers etc. But all this is no good to deaf people unless they have the language that will enable them to take out all this information and put it into their heads. Being unable to understand English grammar makes them dependent on hearing people who make a career out of 'helping' them, and pseudo deaf people who would like to keep the status quo.

Also, there is a lot of money involved in sign language classes that promote BSL as the language of deaf people. If we could ask for a sample of a BSL user's writing it would be obvious why most sixteen year old deaf children still leave school with a reading and writing ability of an eight or nine year old hearing child. BSL's grammar is 'unique', or, in other words, 'back to front', so how can a hearing teacher understand a deaf child using BSL, and how can a deaf child using BSL possibly understand a hearing teacher trying to teach using the correct English grammar by the oral method. There is obviously going to be a lot of misunderstanding on both sides. Oralism will only take deaf people out of the deaf world, but it will not put them into the hearing world and they will still be left isolated.

****

Miss Harker taught me how to knit with thick knitting needles and thick wool from an unravelled sweater. It took me, by trial and error, two months to knit a 12 inch by 12 inch square. I can't remember what colour it was, but I was very proud of it and wrapped it up and sent it home. When I went home for the three-week Christmas holiday I looked for it, but I couldn't find it. I thought that it would be on the table with the vase on it, but it wasn't. Then I thought Mam must only bring it out on special occasions. I asked Mam where it was. She told me that it was in the kitchen and she used it for washing the dishes, for which apparently it was perfect. Oh, well! It was only a woollen rag and there were much more important things to be considered, such as what have I got for Christmas? I cannot ever remember being disappointed with my Christmas or birthday presents. Kids of my generation had learned not to expect too much, they were austerity years.

As the Christmas holidays approached we were all getting excited at the prospect of going home and seeing our families again. We would have three whole weeks at home with them. We started counting down the days some time in November. On the day of our journey home we were all assembled in the playroom;

we had our going home suits on and we all felt very smart and sophisticated. Some of the bigger boys had smeared their hair with brylcream and arranged it in waves and their foreheads were shiny with it. I felt grown up with my long trousers on. We had labels with our names and addresses on, in case we got lost, which we had to tie to the button hole in our jackets, and it quite spoiled the sophisticated image that I was trying to cultivate. Each of us also had a packet of sandwiches. There were three coaches to take us to Leeds railway Station, where we were split up into three groups, those going south and to London, then the ones going north and to Newcastle, and lastly, the ones going to Liverpool, Manchester and other parts of Lancashire.

Going home for the holidays was a very happy time for us. Unlike the hearing kids who stayed at home all the time, we seemed to experience the extremes of emotion, very happy to be going home, then very sad to be going back to St John's. Going home on the train we were so excited and hyperactive, jumping up and down, unable to sit still for a few minutes and opening the windows and sticking our heads out. If we were going through a tunnel when we stuck our heads out, we ended up with soot all over our faces. We must have made it very hard for the sister who was in charge of us.

During this Christmas holiday I was playing outside with Ken one day when Barney walked past. I said, "Hiya Barney. How are you?" He gave me a wary look, nodded his head and quickly walked away. I was hurt by that attitude and Ken must have seen it because he said, "Never mind him, Kev. Come on here, you can have another go on my bike." I had been told by the sisters that Protestants were bad people, and to keep away from them or else they would lead me astray, but that was clearly wrong because Ken and his family were lovely people, they spoke very clearly and were very easy for me to lip read. I decided then that I would make my own mind up about whom I was friends with.

After the Christmas holidays, back in school again, it would be seven long months before we would be going home for the summer holidays as we had to stay in the school for the Easter holiday.

Miss Harker had decided to teach us Morris dancing. We had to put these silly hats on and put bells round our legs and wave coloured cloths about. She would whack us on our legs with a cane if we didn't lift them high enough, all good clean fun, and very instructive, but it put me off dancing for the rest of my life! That's why when at dances or parties you can usually find me propping up the bar! She entered us into a dancing competition with some other schoolchildren from the surrounding village schools and the winners of this dancing competition would win a lovely trophy. She was exhorting us to train harder and telling us that we would be very proud if we won this trophy, but actually none of us wanted to be in the dancing team, so we were trying to be bad dancers so that we wouldn't be picked. I heaved a sigh of relief when I wasn't selected to dance for the school. I was certainly no twinkle toes, I was more like a carthorse, and it would have been embarrassing for me to be seen trying to be a dancer.

Sometimes she would take the class for a walk, and anything that would take us out of the school environs was always welcomed by the boys. The walk usually led us in a roundabout way to her house, which was in the village of Clifford, where she would invite us in and make us clean up her house and garden, and, as a reward, she would give us some cake and lemonade. Sister Teresa, however, would take us on more interesting walks, down by the River Wharfe and Jackdaw Crag.

An important lesson that we were taught by the sisters was to know our lowly status in the hierarchy of the place. If we met any adult or VIPs anywhere in the institution, as they were our betters we had to stand to attention as they passed us, and depending on our age we had to give them either the wolf cub or scout salute to show them respect.

From the age of ten we were taught trade skills after school. Tailoring was taught by Mr Beercock, who made a show of hating the Irish and would stick a needle into the bums of boys with Irish names when he could catch us unawares. Any new boy to his class was always asked what his name wass, and if it was Murphy or O'Neil or some other Irish name he would look heavenwards and say, "O Lord help me, another Irish Bastard". he always said this with a smile on his face, so it was hard to tell if he was serious about it or not, and trusting soul that I was, I used to get the needle in my bum quite a lot, "Political Correctness" was something that nobody had ever heard of in those days.

We were taught Carpentry by Mr Harker, Miss Harker's brother and a very quiet man. Shoemaking and repairing was don by Mr Carroll, Working in the vegetable garden by Mr Shann and helping on the farm by Farmer Dawson. The older boys over the age of fourteen were 'allowed' to help the farmer pick potatoes at harvest time, which was back-breaking work which they shouldn't have made young boys do. I remember once, in my first year at St John's, the big boys had been potato picking. I was not old enough to do it yet, but these big boys came trudging wearily back from the farm looking absolutely shattered. Farmer Dawson had given the money due to them to Sister Catherine so that she could give it to them. They accepted their wages meekly, but one of the big boys, whom I learned later was named John Spearing, looked at the half crown in his hand with disgust on his face, and, with a curl on his upper lip, said to Sister Catherine, "Is that all we get for breaking our backs all week?" Sister Catherine just looked at him and didn't know what to say. Maybe she was thinking, 'There's always an awkward one'. John Spearing stormed off to the farm to sort it out with farmer Dawson, and after a while he came back. We all gathered around him with our eyes agog and our mouths open, eager to know what had happened at the farm. He told us that he had hammered on the door and Farmer Dawson wouldn't open it. Instead, he opened an upstairs window and asked what was going on. John Spearing told Farmer Dawson that he was going to write to the 'Yorkshire Post' about this slave labour and he was shouting and ranting outside the farmhouse and wouldn't shut up. In the end the farmer came out and gave him another half crown and that satisfied him. When I was old enough to go potato picking the pay was five shillings (25p) a week thanks to John Spearing!

I enjoyed riding on the big shirehorse as it pulled the cart full of potatoes back to the farm at the end of the day. My legs were split right out sideways, almost like doing the splits, because the horse was so massive. They were very strong and such gentle, patient, big animals, I couldn't help loving them. There were some German prisoners of war who worked on the farm, too, though I don't know how much they were paid for their work, or if they were paid at all. There were no soldiers with rifles guarding them; they wore coloured patches on their jackets so that people knew they were prisoners of war. I suppose that at that period in history it was better for them to be in Britain than home in war-ravaged Germany so they had no desire to escape.

Farmer Dawson was a very corpulent man. He had a big, round and very red face, and he had an extremely wide girth. One day, when he came into the tailor shop to be measured for a pair of breeches, the tape measure wouldn't fit round his waist. It took two people to measure him; one boy would hold the end of the tape measure and Mr Beercock, the tailor, would walk round him and mark where the tape measure ended with a piece of chalk on his trousers and measure from that mark again. After he had gone, Mr Beercock said that he would show me how to mark and cut the cloth for Farmer Dawson's breeches. I thought, 'Blimey! I hope there's enough cloth – his waist measurement was way over sixty inches. Farmer Dawson looked really funny as he rode back to the farm on his rickety little bike and I wondered how such a delicate-looking object could bear his weight – he must have weighed well over twenty stone! The only concession that he had made was to replace the bike's saddle with a seat from one of the old tractors, a normal bike saddle must have been very painful for him.

There was a little hunched-over old deaf man, who had long thin wispy snowy-white hair that hung down the back of his neck over his shirt collar with his pink scalp showing through, and who always had a pair of spectacles perched on the end of his rather long and red hooked nose. Mr Whecker was his name and he was always in the printing shop, which was situated over the tailor's. None of the boys were ever taught the printing trade by Mr Whecker. In my time at St John's, he rarely came out of this shop and I don't think anybody ever saw him come in or go home. Another of his duties, and one of the rare times that we ever saw him, was when he cut the boys' hair. He had very pale watery-blue eyes and a long thin red nose and always seemed to have an icicle of snot hanging down from the end of it like a stalactite. It was the same even in summer, he was always sniffing it up, but it always came down on the end of his nose again. He was fighting a losing battle with it and I don't know why he never wiped his nose with a handkerchief, or even wiped his nose on his coat sleeve.

The unfortunate boy who was in the barber's chair was always trying to keep his nose in sight, apprehensively hoping the snot wouldn't drip off Mr Whecker's nose and onto his head. If it did, Mr Whecker would just rub it in as if it was hair cream, along with lots of the essential oils that would give a shine to the boy's hair. All this moving about and fidgeting by the boys trying to evade Mr Whecker's snot led to some terrible haircuts. He would smack us on the head and tell us to keep still, sniffing all the time. He used a pair of hand clippers and he tended to pull the hair out rather than cut it. I would always ask him to cut my hair like Alan Ladd's, but he never took any notice of what I or any other boy said to him; we all had the same haircut, very short all round with little islands or tufts of

My sister Patricia on the left, without whom I would never
have been able to read and write properly, and my Mam
and Dad on the right in the middle of what seems
like a long session in the pub!

Auntie Ruth in typical spiv mode at the wheel of a car,
with Aunti Mary on the far right, my Mam next to her
and my Auntie Elsie standing at the back.

Above: The front entrance of St. John's Institution for the Deaf and Dumb.

Below: The side view from the football field.

Above: The farmhouse looking shabby in 2009.

Below: The chapel on the right and the boys' classrooms and dormitory on the left.

Photo taken in 1950 after a sports rally.
Left to right, back row: Mr Ryan, Tony Vaux, Peter Bell,
Val Adamus, John Dolan, Cyril Clarke, Fr. Ronchetti,
Colin Dyer, Me, Michael O'Shea, Miss Smith,
Mr Arthur Young. Front row: Edward Francis, Willie Kelly,
Hugh Dwyer, John Baker.

We won the St John Ambulance Shield for first aid under
Mr Caproni's tutorage. Left to right: Cyril Clarke, Me,
Colin Dyer and Willie Kelly.

Football Team of 1949-50 season. Left to right, back row:
Mr Young, Willie Kelly, Roger Stevens, Cyril Clarke, Me,
Danny Moynihan, Con Lynch, Front row: Kenneth Aspin,
Wally Adamus, Billy Jones, Brian Kelly, John Wilson, Hugh
Dwyer. We were League Champions and beat all-comers.

Sister Margaret, Sister Teresa, Sister Gabriel, Sister Kevin
and Sister Barbara. I've not got much to say about them.

Above: Graves of pupils and Sisters at St Edwards
in Clifford. Some are of past pupils who wished to be
buried there near the only place where they had friends.

Below: Entrance to the institute's private cemetery at the farm.

Mr John Caproni – He, too, was deaf and an ex pupil of
St John's, but he had the advantage of a further private
education after he left. He came back to St John's and
became a teacher. He was sorely missed after his death.

With Diana in 1954. We met at Father Hayward's club at 431 Chester Road and have been married now for more than 50 years.

hair here and there and a bigger tuft at the front, presumably for Sister Margaret to grab hold of. We must have been the first ever skinheads! Our hair was only allowed to grow to normal length when the school holidays were near and we would soon be going home. I remember he slipped up once when he cut some boy's hair really short when the summer holidays were just two weeks away, which wasn't enough time for it to grow back to normal, and when Sister Margaret saw what he had done she nearly had a heart attack. Her face was red and her cheeks were wobbling as she berated him in front of the playroom full of boys. She thought that those boys' parents would think that they had nits and the school was infested. As you can envisage, having our hair cut by Mr Whecker was not an experience that we looked forward to with any delight.

Poor Mr Whecker, we felt sorry for him, because despite the terrible haircuts that he gave us, and the way we used to make fun of him, we were very fond of him. He was deaf, like us, and we did not like the way he was being treated, because really, he was a harmless old man. Mr Whecker was an ex pupil of St John's and as a printer his English was excellent, which has made me think that the education of the deaf children by deaf teachers in his time must have been much better than our education by hearing teachers in our time. So the deaf children taught by the modern oral system had no chance of being taught the printing trade.

At St John's Institution for the Deaf and Dumb [sic] we were considered incapable of being taught the National Curriculum, so we were not expected to sit for any examinations and when the inspectors came, the profoundly deaf children were kept at the back out of the way. I'm surprised the inspectors never noticed what was going on. The eleven plus was thought to be far too difficult for us, and any well-paid job in management or the professions was deemed to be far beyond our abilities. When we left St John's we were expected to work with our hands, and any vestiges of spirit or originality were knocked out of us as soon as possible. We were expected to conform and obey and do what we were told to do, and as there were a lot of lads there who didn't understand what they were being told to do, there were many confused little boys. Any vestiges of pride and self confidence that we may have had were soon lost by this dismal failure to give us deaf children a decent education. Whatever they were trying to teach us, it certainly wasn't self-confidence and pride in ourselves!

I don't know where they went wrong with me. Maybe when listening at the bedroom door to my Dad and Uncles Dick and Frank I had absorbed some of their Irish rebel spirit. I had a feeling that Sister Margaret and Sister Teresa had taken an instant dislike to me, but I don't suppose that I was the only boy who had that feeling. They needn't have worried because the feeling was mutual and I tried to keep out of their way as much as possible. We were also told by Sister Teresa that we must marry a good Catholic girl, preferably an Irish girl, and that she must not be deaf because we must have lots of good Catholic children and deafness in the parents was looked upon as one of the chief causes of deafness in the children, which was a ridiculous statement because 90% of deaf children had hearing parents. We were told that to marry a protestant girl would be a mortal sin. Such marriages were known as mixed marriages, and if you did something as unspeakable as that you would be kicked out of the Catholic Church forever with no hope of ever going to Heaven.

It seems amazing today when I look back with horror and disgust that such ridiculous ideas were inflicted on innocent children's minds. Didn't those people realise what they were doing? Didn't they know that they were poisoning those little deaf kids' minds and spoiling their characters for the rest of their lives? It is one thing to be taught something and quite another thing to actually learn it. When you learn something it becomes a permanent part of you, especially when you have worked out what you have learnt by yourself. A lot of what we were taught at St John's just didn't make sense, or at least to me it didn't – I don't know about the other lads. Lessons from the Old Testament, such as 6,000 years ago God made the world in six days and God said "Let there be light" and suddenly there was light – were we really expected to believe that and ignore the fact that there were dinosaurs on the earth millions of years ago? And the sun which gives us light was created only 6,000 years ago. Surely when God said "Let there be light" he meant, "Let there be enlightenment". Well, I think that God gave us brains to use and think with, not to blindly follow such ridiculous dogma. Strangely, there are many people today who still believe all that. Luckily, because of the communication problem a lot of the boys didn't understand what they were being taught.

Because I came from Manchester, Sister Teresa took me to one side and advised me to never go to Father Hayward's Deaf club and church, which I had never heard of at the time and which apparently was on Chester Road in Manchester. She said: "Kevin, keep away from the deaf people in Manchester, especially Fr. Hayward's club. Don't go there, keep well away; find a nice hearing Irish girl and marry her and have lots of children and bring them up to be good Catholics." I found out years later that Fr. Hayward had disagreed with the practice of Mass nearly every morning and all the prayers that the children had to do, and this had antagonised many of the sisters. This was strange because Fr. Hayward was far above them in the hierarchy of the Catholic Church. Did this lack of respect for him have something to do with the fact that he was deaf? I think that Fr. Hayward was a far better priest than Canon Wilson, who seemed to me to be rather stupid, but, of course, he could hear. Because Sister Teresa had told me to keep away from Fr. Hayward's church and deaf club, I resolved that one of the first things that I would do when I left St John's was to find out where it was and to go there, and it was there that I first met my future wife, Diana Taylor. The first time I saw Diana she quite literally took my breath away. I thought she was so beautiful, so in a rather quixotically fateful way I have Sister Teresa to thank for that, though that very clearly was not her intention.

At St John's, among Sister Teresa's duties was to be in charge of the sweet shop. Any money that we had was to be given to her and she would enter in a book how much each boy had. Some boys had plenty of money, some had none, so she would take money from those who could afford it and put it in the names of the boys who had none. Every Sunday was sweet day, and after dinner we would queue up to receive our ration of sweets. They were only cheap sweets, such as sherbet dabs, liquorice laces, bulls eyes or aniseed balls, the sort of sweets that kids love. We looked forward to our weekly ration of sweets and being in charge of the sweet shop made Sister Teresa popular with the boys. She would often fill her pocket with aniseed balls or other sticky sweets and give them out to boys who had been good or who were her favourites, usually boys who had been at St John's from a very early age – some boys had been there since the age of two. Sometimes she would send a boy to fetch something for her, such as her knitting which she had left in the classroom, and as a reward for that boy she would reach into her pocket for a sweet. It was a very deep pocket and she would reach deep into it, way past her knees, bending over to reach the far recesses, searching around for a sweet among all the other things there, and then she would pull out one covered in fluff and dirt and give it to the boy. My Auntie Winnie would send me a 2/6 postal order every month, so I knew that I had plenty in her book. When the time came to go home for the summer or winter holidays, we were given what money was left in our names. I was always given 2/6, never more and never less.

For a lot of us our true education began after we had left St John's. In my own case I have my sister Patricia to thank. She taught me a lot that would be hard for a deaf person to comprehend, such as the pronouncing of words. Words are not always pronounced as they are written, and sometimes English seems to be very illogical to people who cannot hear it spoken. Hearing people can pronounce words correctly because they can hear the words spoken, and so can copy the right way to pronounce them. It is not because they are more intelligent than deaf people, as many seem to think. Deafness is often called the 'Hidden Disability' because there may be no visual clues that the deaf person has a severe hearing loss. Profoundly deaf people don't wear hearing aids. A deaf person's speech may sound strange, they cannot control the volume of their voice, they may pronounce words in a strange way, and some deaf people have learnt to speak never having heard a word. Our Pat was very patient with me and she also instilled in me the love of books, and I have had a passion for them ever since.

****

To return to my first day at St John's, there were four dormitories: St Gabriel's was for the little ones, St Michael's was for the seven to nine year olds, St Joseph's was for the bigger boys, the ten to fourteen year olds and the Sacred Heart was for the biggest boys. I was assigned to St Michael's dormitory. There were about twenty five iron beds in rows. I took off my clothes and put them on the chair that was beside the bed, then I picked up my pyjamas, but before I could put them on I realised that some of the boys were staring at me. One of the bigger boys, who could hear and speak a little, came over to me and told me that I must never take all my clothes off like that or I would get into trouble with Sister Teresa because it was immodest and low and a sin to do that. I must cover myself up and not let the others see my willie and bum. I quickly put my pyjamas on and jumped into the bed that had been assigned to me. All the other boys were sitting up in bed waving their arms about and making strange gestures. I was in an alien world and I wanted to go home. I wanted my Mam and Dad, Jimmy and Pat. I prayed silently to Jesus and promised that if I could go home I would never be naughty again and would always do what I was told to do. That first night at St John's I cried myself to sleep.

Next morning I was jarred out of sleep by Sister Teresa picking up the end of my bed and banging it down. She went on to do the same to some other boys. For a moment I didn't know where I was, but soon it all came flooding back. I had been sent to a strange place where everyone waved their arms about and gesticulated in a strange way. I had no time to feel homesick because Sister Teresa was hurrying us all up. "Come on, come on, hurry up, mustn't be late for Mass, hurry up." I followed the other boys into the washroom, where there were two rows of wash basins. We brushed our teeth but there was no toothpaste. There were some blocks of a hard green soap and we used that for toothpaste and washed our hands and faces with it too, then we dressed in green corduroy shorts, grey woollen jumpers and sandals. All the children were wearing the same type of clothing. Then we had to go to the Chapel where Canon Wilson said Mass. The Mass was said in the old fashioned way, in Latin, and Canon Wilson had his back to us so we couldn't see what was going on. Sometimes, when Sister Teresa was in the pew right behind me on my right side, I could hear a faint, mesmerising murmur: "HolyMary murrer o God,prayferus sinnersnowanatdeourofourdeafamen". She was chanting her prayers automatically, as if in a trance, which she well may have been, and it made me feel very sleepy, as if she was hypnotising me.

I found out that the Institution was run on military lines; we had to assemble in lines and when the order was given with a flick of his arms by Mr Young, which meant "Right turn", we had to turn smartly and march on the spot, arms swinging, knees high, as rank by rank the boys moved into Chapel in single file. The same procedure was followed when going into the refectory for meals, or going to the classrooms and dormitories.

When Mass was over Sister Margaret got up and spoke to us. Most of the boys didn't know what she was saying, but thanks to that extra year at St Malachi's, when I picked up the rudiments of lip-reading, I could pick up most of what she was saying. She said that as a special treat we would all assemble in the hall where Canon Wilson would sing 'Santa Lucia' for us. I'm not sure but I think that it must have been in honour of some Saint's feast day, so we were all marched to the hall and were made to stand there patiently in military-style rank and file while Canon Wilson sang in a thin nasal voice a song that none of the children could hear. Is this what is meant by the 'Oral Method'?

I couldn't hear him either and he was much too far away to lip read, but from his appearance, he was a very thin man with a thin face, thin effeminate hands and fingers which he waved about as he sang. He was certainly no Paul Robeson, so in my mind's ear he had a thin reedy voice. People talk about seeing things in their mind's eye, so why couldn't I call on my memory of when I could hear and hear things in my mind's ear? As a kid I always had a very vivid imagination. When he was finished we had to applaud and thank him. I wondered if I had been sent to an institution for the insane by mistake. Was I, an eight year old boy, the only one who could see how utterly ridiculous it was. Some of the boys enjoyed Canon Wilson's singing. It provided them with enough material for them to mimic his facial expressions and mime his actions as he was singing, and have a laugh about it for days afterwards. I often wonder if my childhood experiences of these 'experts', the Ewings of Manchester University, Canon Wilson, Sister Margaret, Sister Teresa, etc., and also growing up at a time when people and countries were trying to annihilate each other, helped to make me the sceptic that I am today. Nowadays, I have found out that the best way round a problem is to ask a so called 'expert' or 'Guru' in the field, listen to the advice, and then do exactly the opposite – it seems to work for me!

The best teachers are the ones who themselves have lived the life they are talking about. There's nothing worse to me than someone quoting great passages of wisdom, only to realise that this person has never even done what he is telling me to do. I will heed the doers, not the tellers. How can these hearing teachers who cannot sign possibly understand and get inside the minds of deaf children and so be able to teach them? What we needed was some teachers who were deaf themselves, who could understand what it was like to be deaf and be able to communicate fully with the deaf children. Many deaf children are very intelligent, they just need someone who can draw out that intelligence and nurture it.

I remember that I was not always satisfied with the teachers answers to my questions. Looking back now I can recall asking the teachers questions all the time, maybe because having lost one of my senses and having to rely only on my sense of sight for gathering in information, and having such an inquisitive mind, I was trying to make up for that loss. I must have been very irritating to some of the teachers with my constant questioning, but I wanted to understand the world I lived in and what made it go round. Answers such as "It's God's will" didn't make sense to me. I may be wrong but looking back, I think that the education system of the time, and maybe today too, puts too much emphasis on memory. What I mean by that is memorising things and learning by rote, instead of reasoning things and thinking problems out for yourself. I suppose that is what deaf children have to do all the time, being unable to understand most of what the teachers are saying.

I sometimes wonder if the teachers that we had were the ones who didn't qualify to teach in hearing schools, and so were sent to Deaf schools where it didn't really matter because we were considered incapable of sitting for any examinations anyway. Surely it would have been easier for these teachers to learn to sign and so be able to communicate with the children that they were supposed to be educating, rather than expect the children who couldn't hear or speak to understand what the teachers were saying. They were the teachers so the onus should be on them to make sure that the children understood what they were saying.

I never cease to be appalled when looking back at how the teachers were exhorting the deaf kids to "make something of themselves" when they leave St John's. These kids were not even equipped with the right language to say what they want to be when they leave, so how on earth can they "Make it". I should explain here that when I speak of conversations that I have with the other boys it must be understood that we are using sign language to communicate. It didn't take me long to pick up sign language, so surely it would be easy for an adult to learn it. I know that I keep harping on about the 'Oral System' and the bad old days but I feel strongly about it and it has blighted so many deaf kids' lives. Nowadays teachers of the deaf are highly skilled and excellent signers and they are turning out better educated deaf children.

After Canon Wilson's song we were marched to the refectory for breakfast. After we had said grace we were given breakfast, which consisted of a bowl of porridge and a slice of bread and margarine and a cup of watery tea; then, after breakfast we had to give thanks to our Lord for providing us with food. I am sure that if Charles Dickens could have seen us, it would have given him an idea for a book, maybe a sequel to Oliver Twist. When I read the part in Oliver Twist where the children ate gruel, I remembered the porridge at St John's and wondered if Charles Dickens meant porridge? Was gruel an old fashioned name for porridge? The food was very stodgy, filled with carbohydrates and very little protein. Of course, at the time I didn't understand about carbohydrates, proteins and fats, but now I do and in retrospect I can understand that we were being robbed of the rations that everybody was entitled to.

Embedded into my memory of those times is the sight of Sister Margaret, her face flushed and angry, force-feeding some unfortunate child who couldn't stomach the goo we were expected to eat. She would get a spoonful of it, then pinch the child's nose closed and wait for him to open his mouth to breathe. Then she would jam it into his mouth, and then hold his mouth closed. The poor child had to swallow or suffocate. Many years later, when I was an adult, I acquired a copy of the school report in which it said that the wartime menu for the children included such things as roast beef, boiled beef, minced meat pies, Irish stew, fish, chickens etc. That is not as I remember it, and I am sure that any boy of that time would agree with me that it is not true. Maybe the printer, Mr Whecker, put the priests', sisters' and teachers' menu in by mistake. If you look at any old photos of the period you would notice how thin and skinny the children looked compared to the children of today. We were underweight, especially our legs. Then look at the sisters and teachers, so round-faced and well fed.

It seems to me that we live in a society that is based on lies and mistakes, especially so when writing history. On my journey through life I have realised that we all make mistakes but wise people learn from their mistakes. In fact, we learn more from our mistakes than from our successes, except, that is, teachers of the deaf, who carry on making the same mistake year after year. Success is often bestowed on us by the grace of God, or by a lucky accident, whereas on the other hand failure usually happens because you either misjudged the situation, or the character of the people you were dealing with, or you were operating with inaccurate or incomplete information. This is happening all the time with deaf people, who because of bad education are unable to access much information from books, computers etc. I suppose that it is easy to recall what you did wrong when it is over and avoid the same mistake next time, and so we blunder through and get there in the end.

Britain was being blockaded by the German U-boats and food was scarce, but every body was entitled to so much meat, eggs, cheese etc., even if very little. The only time that we saw an egg was at Easter when we were given a boiled egg each. Often, when Sister Margaret was leading us in prayer, we could see small bits of egg yolk in the corner of her mouth where she hadn't wiped it off, which was all the proof that I and the other boys who worked in the vegetable garden needed. So, after talking it over among ourselves, we decided to do something about it. It was a simple matter to slip over to the farm when Mr Shann had gone off for a cigarette. We would search for eggs in the haystacks as the chickens at the farm were free to wander around and they laid eggs in the haystacks where they had built their nests, whilst the ducks would lay their eggs anywhere. We would gather about a dozen eggs and boil them in a can of water in the boiler house. Cyril once said that it was a sin to steal and we couldn't be forgiven until we had given back what we had stolen, but needs must. Anyway, Cyril ate his share. How could we give back what we had eaten? We would worry about forgiveness later; after all, they were stealing our rations and many of the children were aware of that too.

Once a lad named Roger and I were in the boiler house. We had opened the door of the boiler to get at the red hot glowing embers to boil the water can with about six eggs in and make some toast with bread that we had saved from breakfast. After we had scoffed it all we went up the stairs to the exit, but as luck would have it, Mr Young caught us as we were leaving. The boiler room was out of bounds to any children. He reported us to Sister Margaret and we were sent separately to her office to be questioned. I managed to sign to Roger, "Don't mention the eggs, just toast." Roger winked that he understood. Sister Margaret didn't believe that we were in the boiler house to make toast; she was convinced that we were doing filthy, unmentionable things to each other, and so Mr Young was sent for to give us ten slaps each on the back of our thighs. I wanted to go home away from this mad house and have some proper food at our house or my Auntie Ruth's. I was sure that Auntie Ruth and my Mam would have been livid if they knew what was going on there.

After breakfast and before we went into the classrooms, we had to assemble in the playroom in ranks and files and say prayers. We had to hold our arms out as we prayed, like Jesus did when he was crucified. This is the time when we usually saw the egg yolk on Sister Margaret's mouth. After school, at twelve o'clock, it was dinner time. First we had to say prayers before our meal. Dinner usually consisted of a stew of vegetables and a pudding of semolina, sago or, rarely, a rice pudding, then another prayer to give thanks to Our Lord. Now, I am not exaggerating whwn I tell you we had to say a prayer before play. You may be wondering how deaf kids who were unable to speak and not allowed to use sign language could say their prayers if they had to hold their arms out sideways as if crucified, or join their hands together with fingers pointed heavenwards. The answer is simple: the boys were taught to speak like you would teach a parrot by repeatedly making them pray before and after we did everything, i.e. grace before and after meals, when we woke up in the morning and when we went to bed at night, before school and after school, and before and after play. There were only a limited number of prayers: 'Our Father', 'Hail Mary' and 'Glory Be', as well as Grace before and after meals. The result of this constant praying was that some boys (not all) became expert at saying a few prayers like a parrot but could not hold an ordinary conversation with their families or other hearing people. They would copy the sister or teacher in charge who would recite them. I am sure that many boys were thinking of other things than prayers! I will not mention the prayers that we had to say anymore, the reader can assume that before any activity we had to say a prayer.

At last we were allowed to play out. I was quite good at football so I was allowed to play with boys who were older than me. There were three football fields, and they were given numbers; field number 1st and 2nd was for the big boys, 3rd and 4th was for the smaller boys and 5th and 6th was for the little kids.

****

And so I settled in and became resigned to life at St John's Institution for the Deaf and Dumb. I don't know how the girls passed their time at St John's, but I imagine it was much the same as us boys. I often wondered how Nora was coping, but I only ever saw her out of the corner of my eye in Chapel when she was going past for Holy Communion. The boys and girls were kept strictly apart and we were not allowed to even look at them never mind speak to them. We did manage to get some words across from a distance – that's the beauty of sign language – "What's your name?" or "Hello, I'm Kevin", "No. Not Kiven, Kevin!" It was Mass and prayers, Benediction and prayers and more prayers. Please don't get me wrong, I am a big believer in the power of prayers, Praying is embedded deep into the Irish psych, but not when prayers are made compulsory. Prayers must come from your heart, you must really mean them. Prayers are a form of positive thinking. Praying helps to give you confidence and it calms you, but it's no good if you are just reciting your prayers parrot-fashion because you have been told to do so. Anyway, I am sure that most of the boys were thinking of anything else but prayers as I know that I used to drift off into a dream world.

At Mass the boys had to sit in the front pews and the girls in the back pews where we couldn't see them. When the girls went past us to receive Holy communion we had to look away; there was always a sister there watching us to make sure that we didn't ogle them or send them messages silently by sign language, which was easily done if the sisters were not alert and watchful all the time. Even at that tender young age I thought it was ridiculous. What possible harm would it do for us to talk to the girls? It was the most natural thing in the world for boys and girls to play and talk together. These Sisters were acting as if we were slavering perverts and sex maniacs and the girls were innocent virgins whose virtue must be protected at all costs.

We had to go to confession every Saturday so that we could receive Holy Communion with a clean soul on Sunday. We would write our confessions on a piece of paper and hand it to Canon Wilson in the confessional. With all the praying and the sisters monitoring our every movement, the chances for us to commit any big or interesting sins was very limited, and I for one was not going to confess to stealing eggs from the farm or they would have put a stop to it. So to make it worthwhile going into confession we would make some sins up and try to outdo each other. One boy once wrote: "I had low thoughts ten times", so I wrote "I had low thoughts twelve times", then another boy would see what I had written and he would write that he had *very* low thoughts fifteen times and he had touched his willie. I am not surprised that Canon Wilson had an expression of long-suffering hopelessness on his face in the confessional. To help to fill in the paper with my confession on it I would sometimes write, "I looked at the girls eight times". Canon Wilson never told me that this was not a sin. Then Canon Wilson would write the penance for us: three 'Hail Marys', two 'Our Fathers' and one 'Glory Be'. The penance was invariably the same for us all, no matter how many times we had been "low" or touched ourselves where we shouldn't. Were all these mistakes and misunderstandings due to the fact that he couldn't communicate fully with the children? Some of the boys couldn't read or write and they would ask me or another lad to write their confessions for them. They would then make a copy of it and use the same one every week. I wondered if Canon Wilson ever noticed so many confessions were identical. Was he even bothered?

At first I didn't know what was meant by using the word "low" in that context, but later I was to learn that "low" meant "Sex", although this word was taboo and was never to be mentioned. To the sick minds of these religious bigots, sex meant just touching yourself in that unmentionable part of your own body; it was a mortal sin if you did and you were condemned to suffer everlasting fire in hell unless you confessed your sin. Sister Margaret would lecture us most nights before bed that we must sleep on our backs with our arms crossed on our chests, never lie on your stomach or on your side with your hands between your legs. I suppose that she thought that it would awaken licentious feelings in us. I couldn't help thinking that God had made a mistake when he made us. Why did He give us parts of our bodies that it was a sin to touch? And why did He make boys and girls different? I noticed that Sisters Margaret and Teresa were particularly hard on any boy who was good looking (Me!), and when talking to some of the girls years later after we had left St John's I was told that any pretty girl was picked on by the sisters. A wise man once said, "Every society is judged by how it treats the least fortunate amongst them". That statement speaks volumes to me.

I was a light sleeper but some of the boys were very heavy sleepers, one boy in particular. I will call him Don to save him from embarrassment if he is still alive, and if he ever reads this he will know who I am writing about and I hope, thank me, for not using his real name. Don was a very heavy sleeper, I am sure that he could sleep through an earthquake. So Sister Margaret would always grab the blankets on Don's bed and pull them off him and shake him awake – until one morning when she pulled the blankets off Don and there it was, in full view of us all in all it's majesty, standing at attention, one of the best morning glories that dormitory had ever witnessed. At first Sister Margaret drew back with a shocked look, her face was white and her eyes were bulging. Then she went red with anger as she stood there looking at it. Don was still fast asleep, probably having a nice dream, blissfully unaware of the shock he was giving Sister Margaret, who then started slapping Don across his face. Poor Don, to be awakened like that by a mad woman. It must have been an experience that he would never forget. It must have been traumatic for Sister Margaret too, because after that she never again pulled the blankets off Don or anybody else. An experience like that could easily have given her a heart attack! From that day on she copied Sister Teresa's method of picking up the end of the bed and banging it down. That is one of the most enduring memories that I have about St John's and I will remember it always. Whenever I am feeling sad and need to lighten my mood, I think of Sister Margaret's facial expression when she pulled the blankets off Don exposing his massive erection, and I immediately have a laugh and feel my mood lightening (evil laughter).

At first I couldn't receive Holy Communion because, even though I had made my first Holy Communion at St Malachi's, the Sister Superior Sister Catherine didn't believe me when I told her that I had, so I had to make a second "First" Holy Communion. I didn't mind because the first Holy Communicants had a party with fruit cake and lemonade.

I made friends with one of the boys named Cornelius Lynch (Con for short), who had the bed next to me in St Michael's dormitory. He showed me how to communicate by signing. First he taught me the alphabet, then he would spell out slowly on his fingers words like "Bum", "Poo", "Pee" and "Willie" etc. When I got it there would be gales of inane laughing and giggling. We thought that we were so daring for using such bad words! Then he would teach me the signs for the words that I had spelled out, and as it was the only way that we could communicate I soon picked it up. Was Con the first sign language tutor? Con told me that he and his big brother Free (Humphrey), who was also deaf and at St John's, came from Cork in Ireland and they hadn't been home for four years because of the war. Con was at St John's for a total of eleven years. Imagine that, a little kid taken from his loved ones and incarcerated in that place for that long. He and his brother never once went home for the holidays, even when the war was over he still had to stay for another five years until he finally left at the age of sixteen in 1950. For two brothers to be born deaf must mean that it was a genetic defect in the family, which is very rare. In fact, 90% of deaf children come from hearing families, so there goes Sister Teresa's theory that deaf couples should not have children because they will be born deaf. Con and Free must have been strangers to their family when they finally went home. It's hard to imagine that they were successfully integrated into the family home after so long away. That was another thing that those Jerries had to answer for.

Gradually, as my signing skills improved so my circle of friends grew, or should I say my companions in wretchedness, because I don't think that any of the boys at St John's were truly happy. How could they be expected to be happy when they were taken from their families and loved ones and dumped into such a repressive environment? The strict regime of prayers with Mass five times a week and Benediction three times a week and punishments for the slightest infringement of the rules, of which there were many, was enough to break anybody's spirit. If they imagined that it would make us good people, whiter than white, when we left St John's then they were very badly mistaken. Most of us ended up being alcoholics and misfits. I know for a fact that one alumni worked his way up to be one of the hit men in the London underworld. Most of us found it very hard to fit into the hearing world.

I well remember one religious lesson given at Easter time by Sister Margaret about the crucifixion of Jesus. She was saying that Christ died in agony on the cross to save wretches like "You... and you... and you". Her eyes were bulging and her jowls were shaking as she glared and pointed at each of us in turn. And when our Lord was dying of thirst on the cross did they give him water? No, they gave him vinegar, "VINEGAR!" she shouted, not water but vinegar. How cruel is that! She was banging her desk to add emphasis to her words and she seemed to be glaring right at me as she spoke, as if it was my fault entirely. I wonder how many kids had guilt complexes after lessons like that.

By the time most of the boys were of leaving age they had already had enough religion crammed into them to last them for several lifetimes. The Sister Superior, Sister Catherine, had recently retired and Sister Margaret had taken over the duties of the Sister Superior, which is when conditions began to get worse. The main rule, which seemed to be an obsession with Sister Margaret, was that we must not look at the girls, because if we did it would give us "low" thoughts. At St John's the boys and girls were strictly segregated, the apartheid government of South Africa was nothing compared to Sister Margaret's regime at St John's. If caught looking at the girls, or breaking the rules in any other way, Mr Young was called to administer the punishment. We all wore short trousers and he would pull up our trouser leg and smack us on the back of our thighs, the number of smacks depending on the severity of the "offence".

Mr Young was the 'school' caretaker and odd job man and his hands were large and hard and hurt us a lot. The sister in charge would watch the punishment, sometimes with a smile on her face, as the unfortunate boy was squirming and screaming.

I remember one day one of the big boys grabbed hold of me, gave me some chalk and twisted my arm as he made me write the words 'F..k Off' on the wall. Then he told another boy to fetch Mr Young. When Mr Young came he told him that he had caught me writing these terrible words. Sister Margaret was sent for and she said that she didn't know what those words meant, but she believed Mr Young when he said they were terrible words and so, despite all my protestations of innocence, I had to be punished. My trouser leg was pulled up and ten smacks were administered on each leg and I was sent to bed with no supper. Some boys were never punished. They were favourites of one or other of the sisters. However, one boy who was never punished was Billy Jones. The reason why he was never punished by Mr Young was not because he was a favourite, but because he was a massive boy for his age. Billy Jones was a one-off; he was bigger than Mr Young and as strong as a horse. I am sure that one blow from him would have sent Mr Young flying into orbit.

The same big boy who got me into trouble never played with the boys his own age; he always played with the little ones on the 3rd and 4th field and he had a lot of fun knocking and pushing them about. I was kicking a ball about in the playground one day when he came up behind me and pushed me over. I hit the ground hard and banged my nose. I rolled over onto my back feeling dazed and swallowing blood. For a moment I just lay there, then I rolled over onto my stomach, wiped the blood from my nose and tried to focus my eyes on my tormentor. I could barely see him through the haze of tears – tears of pain – but much more than that – tears of blind rage. He stood there in front of me, arms akimbo and grinning. I knew that he was too big for me, but nevertheless I pushed myself up and launched myself at him and rammed my head into his stomach. He certainly wasn't expecting that, I knocked the breath out of him. He was lying on the ground doubled over holding his stomach, making a strange moaning sound and trying to get his breath back. Luckily there was no sister about to witness the incident, so I just walked off and left him lying there. I went to the wash toilets and washed the blood from my face. That lad never bothered me again.

I say 'school' from habit but in reality it was an 'institution', which I now realise can be compared to an asylum. That made us 'inmates', not school children. Another meaning of the word 'asylum' is 'sanctuary' or 'safe haven', but in those days St John's was far from a safe place for us children. It seemed to me that we were being punished for being deaf. Although we never went home for the Easter holidays, sometimes our parents would visit us at this time. My Mam and Auntie Ruth came to visit me one Easter. It was great to see them, and after lots of cuddles and kisses they took me for a walk into the village and we had dinner in a café. I answered all their questions: "Yes! We had plenty to eat... Yes! I was happy and had lots of friends." If I told my Mam what it was really like she would either be very upset, and I didn't want that, or she wouldn't believe me. Auntie Ruth was different, she was a real hard case and knew lots of dodgy characters, so I didn't dare to tell her what it was really like as she would have caused a lot of trouble.

Another Easter time a group of old pupils came to visit and I recognised the old deaf man from Collyhurst, who we used to ask for the time. I told him that I knew him from Manchester. The others gathered around me and asked me where I was from. I explained that I was from Manchester, the same as them, and I knew the old man named Arthur Thresh. They told me their names: James Thresh, who was Arthur's brother, Larry Gunning, who wore rimless glasses and looked like an intellectual, Terry Riley and his wife Mary, who were a lovely couple and were always smiling, Christopher Beaden, Bernard McShea and some others whose names I have forgotten. There was a little rotund priest with them. They introduced me to him and told me his name was Father Hayward. I shook hands with them all and Fr. Hayward said that I must go to his club when I left St John's. This was the person that Sister Teresa said I must keep away from. I thought that he was very nice and harmless, so I decided that when I left St John's I would check his club out and make my own mind up.

St John's changed from 'St John's Institution for the Deaf and Dumb' to 'St John's School for Hearing Impaired Children' in 1953, two years after I'd left, when a new priest Canon Kelly was put in charge. As well as changing that awful, demeaning sign, 'St John's Institution for the Deaf and Dumb', Canon Kelly made many more significant changes. For a start, he got rid of all the adult lodgers. They may have had a place in an 'institution', but they had no place in a 'school' for deaf children. Next he got rid of the notion that the deaf were only fit for working with their hands and had to be taught to be good workers worthy of their hire. There is no shame in being a manual worker if that is what you want, but many of the deaf kids had the potential to do much better and to go on to higher education. Canon Kelly could see and understand that, God bless him. He modernised the ancient curricula and shook up the whole education system of St John's, and he gave the children a fighting chance to make good in the outside hearing world. How I wish that he had come to St John's when I was there and not after I had left, but that's the way it goes.

However, before we start erecting statues in his memory, it must be understood that nobody is perfect and that there was a dark side to Canon Kelly. I have been reliably informed by three boys who were there at the time that Canon Kelly was a bad-tempered and insensitive man. He liked to play football with the boys and one day one of the boys jumped up to head a goal from a corner kick and he accidently bumped into Canon Kelly, who was defending, and knocked him over. Canon Kelly was very angry, so he choose to look upon it as an affront to his dignity and sent that boy off, even though he wasn't the referee. One of his hobbies was shooting and he would regularly take three or four boys with him to act as retrievers and bring back the pheasants and partridges or other game that he had shot, much to the amusement of his rich shooting buddies, who used dogs for that task. Afterwards he would sometimes be invited to one of these rich people's houses for dinner, so these boys would have to wait in his car for two or three hours while he was enjoying a good meal and convivial company, just like it was in the middle ages when you had country squires and serfs. Like

I said, nobody is perfect and I am sure that his good qualities outweighed his bad ones.

****

Returning back to my time at St John's, even in this oppressive environment they couldn't stop life and the hormones bubbling away inside us boys, so we came up with a cunning plan. If a boy fancied one of the girls he would write her a letter professing undying love. We had an old tennis ball with a tear in it, so the letter was put into the ball and thrown over the carpentry shop into the girls' playground, where it was found and passed on to the girl named. The girls would do the same, a letter in the ball and the ball thrown back over. It was a good feeling to know that we were putting one over on these insane people who were in charge of us.

All went according to plan for a few weeks, but then one day Cyril asked me to write a letter for him to a girl that he liked. Cyril's English was not very good, mine was good; my maths were not very good, whereas Cyril's maths were brilliant, so we often helped each other. I wrote a very good romantic letter for Cyril professing his undying love and I added some poetry and drew some flowers for good measure. It was duly put into the ball and thrown over the carpentry shop where, as fate would have it, it landed at the feet of the sister in charge. The letter was found and passed on to Sister Margaret. Well that was it! The proverbial had hit the fan. Cyril was caught by Sister Margaret, who had a habit of grabbing misbehaving boys by the tuft of hair that Mr Whecker had left on the front of the boy's heads when he gave us our haircuts. She would grab hold of our hair and swing our heads around, and this she now proceeded to do with gusto to poor Cyril (the canny ones among us put vaseline on our hair). Mr Young was sent for to administer Cyril's punishment, until he told who had written the note for him. In the end Cyril had to tell her it was me, and I couldn't blame him.

Sister Margaret told me later in her office before my punishment that looking at Cyril's snotty nose and the yellow stuff coming from his ears, which cotton wool failed to stop, she just knew that he was incapable of any romantic and flowery words. "Roses are red my dear, violets are blue" and the rest of the song couldn't possibly have been written by Cyril. She said that she suspected that it was me who had written it, though she never said why she suspected me of this heinous crime, and she was determined to make Cyril say who had written such filthy words. She said it in a contemptuous voice and a curl to her upper lip, which just shows the low opinion she had for some of us boys.

I said yes, I had written it, but it was not filthy, I thought it was lovely. She became very angry because I had contradicted her, and eyes narrowed and she had a grim expression on her face as she told me to stand in front of her and put my hands behind my back. When I did so she swung her hand at my face, but I instinctively put my arm up and blocked her slap. This must have hurt her hand because she became even more angry. Her face was red with fury as she shouted in a shrill voice, "How dare you fight back at me." Mr Young was sent for to give me his special punishment on the back of my legs.

Little did she know that her attempts to smother any feelings of love and tenderness amongst the kids had failed – the girls who worked in the laundry were fighting over who could wash the clothes of their favourite boys.

Years later, when thinking about all these incidents, it made me realise that Germany was not the only place where bad things could happen to disabled people; it could easily happen here, or anywhere else. If the wrong people get into positions of power they will abuse it. Here in Britain the government had to make it illegal to discriminate against disabled people and that law was really needed because the discrimination was so bad.

Did you know that Alexander Graham Bell, one of the greatest brains of his time and the inventor of the telephone, said that the deaf were a defective variety of the human race. He tried to stop sign language and to push through laws forbidding marriage between deaf people, as well as compulsory sterilisation of deaf girls. Some states even passed such legislation. St Augustine (354-430) taught that the deaf were excluded from salvation because they couldn't hear the "Word of God". He also taught that handicapped children were the result of the sins of the parents. So it seems that the deaf have been discriminated against for thousands of years, even by such exalted people as St Augustine. Why on earth was he made a Saint? We were taught to pray to such people – my mind boggles at the thought.

One day, as I was messing about in the carpentry shop, the word came for someone to go over to the girls' side to repair a broken window in their bathroom. The carpentry tutor, Mr Harker, gathered his tools together and told me to accompany him and he would show me how to repair a broken window. The plan was that we would put the ladder up and he would go up it to knock out all the broken glass, put it in a bucket, then measure how much glass we needed and go back and cut it. Mr Harker knocked all the glass out, then came down the ladder and said to me, "Kevin, you go up the ladder to see what it is like. Don't be scared, I will hold it steady." So I went up the ladder gingerly, but as I came level with the window the bathroom door suddenly opened and some girls came in. I was just frozen there with my mouth open and my eyes on stalks. I didn't know what to do. The girls were giggling and pointing at me, then the Sister in charge came in. She saw me and came charging over like a mad rhino. I nearly fell off the ladder in my haste to get down.

The incident was reported to Sister Margaret and Mr Young was sent for to administer punishment. Why I was being punished was a mystery to me because the girls were covered up and I was told to go there with Mr Harker. I made a silent vow that when I was a man I would come back and avenge myself, but I never did. I was told by Tom Dullard, an adult deaf man who lodged at St John's, that Mr Young didn't like what he was doing but had to obey orders or he would lose his job and he had a wife and son to think of. He lacked the moral courage to say, "No, I won't do it."

Bullying of the little boys by the bigger boys seemed to be encouraged because when it happened the Sister in charge would just stand by and watch. Maybe they thought that it was character building for the little ones to be bullied by the big ones, I cannot ever remember any Sister telling a big boy to stop bullying a small boy. Some of the bigger boys would arrange fights between the smaller boys, just as if they were boxing managers. Thanks to my Collyhurst upbringing I was handy with my fists and my 'manager' was proud of me because I won many fights. For many years now I have felt bad about the part I played in that shameful charade. The lads who took part in these arranged fights seemed to understand that there was no malice intended. It was looked upon as a sport and not something that we were made to do, so no grudges were ever held.

Once a month we were given a cupful of a concoction made from sennapods. It was there on the table when we went in for breakfast and we had to drink it before we could have any breakfast. It was an evil-smelling brew and tasted awful. It was a laxative and was meant to keep us 'open'. Sometimes Cyril would drink my dose of senna, but only if I promised him my sweet ration on Sunday. On these occasions Sister Margaret was very busy with her force-feeding technique. Now at that time there were about one hundred boys and the institute had only about twelve toilets on the boy's side. You don't need to be very clever to imagine the chaos that ensued. Why did all the boys have to have this senna on the same day? Why not twelve boys at a time, because that was the number of toilets. Some of the little ones couldn't hold it in and did it in their trousers and were punished for it. It was wartime and there was no nice soft toilet paper, we had to use torn up newspaper. We all had black bums from the ink on the newspaper and the toilets would become blocked and overflow and Mr Young would have to come and unblock them. It was a disgusting job for him and so unnecessary if it had been planned properly by the people whom we had to salute and show respect to.

We would have a bath once a week, except after a muddy football game when we had to bathe the muck off. One bathful of water would have to do for six boys before it was changed for fresh water. Not very hygienic, was it? After we had been playing football on the muddy, cow pat-littered field, the water could end up being very muddy indeed; it would have made great liquid feed for plants. I understand how the old saying "Don't throw the baby away with the bath water" originated. I also know that one or two of the boys used to pee in the bath just for the fun of it and I always tried to avoid getting into the bath after them. The sister in charge always combed our hair with a fine tooth comb on these bath days, ostensibly to get rid of nits – it was more likely to spread nits from one boy to another – also, her gaze seemed to linger longer than necessary on some of the boys when they got out of the bath. Other boys had noticed that too, not just me.

In the refectory Sister Philomena arranged a competition between the tables. At the end of the week the children on the table with the cleanest table cloth would win a piece of slab cake each. There were two big boys in charge of each table and their job was to see that the table cloths were spotless at the end of the week. In the middle of each table was a vase of artificial flowers, so when we had finished eating we were made to sit well back from the table with our arms folded and look at the flowers. The big boys in charge (we had to call them 'captains') would patrol round the table watching us, and if our gaze strayed away from the flowers we would get a smack across the face. I had learnt to cry so once I had a smack on my face it seemed to satisfy the 'captain' and he would leave me alone.

Seated next to me at my table was a boy named Denis. One day, for some reason, Denis received a smack on his face but didn't cry. The captain said, "Oh, a tough one" and he gave Denis another smack. Still Denis didn't cry. The captain called another captain over and told him, "I've got a tough one here, he won't cry." The other captain said, "Let me try" and he went up behind Denis and pulled back his arm and swung it at Denis's face from behind with all his might. Denis was knocked flying out of his chair, but still he didn't cry and just got quietly back up and sat down again. Inside I was screaming silently at Denis to cry, "Cry you silly fool", but Denis endured another three or four full force smacks that would knock his head back forcefully before, mercifully, he burst into tears.

Why didn't I do something to stop this awful bullying of poor Denis? Was it cowardice? It was happening right next to me and I did nothing. Despite the fact that these "captains" were four or five years older than me, I feel strongly that I should have tried to stop it. I feel that as I did not protest against it then I was co-operating with it and was just as guilty. When I met some of these bullies years later at the 'Boston Spa reunions', they were sorry for what they had done and explained it as a 'custom' and that they had been bullied when they were little too. Bullying must be happening in hearing schools as well, it just seems much worse in residential schools.

Now that I'm a man, this subject of bullying has been preying on my mind for many years. It fills me with revulsion, and if I see any bullying I will go and stop it. Surely such brutal treatment must have destroyed something inside these little deaf children and the big boys who bullied must have had something inside them destroyed also. I know that I am still affected today by my experiences at St John's so many years ago. For more serious crimes, such as a speck of food marking the table cloth, we would receive a smack across the back of our hands with a large serving ladle. It would make our hands swell up and be sore for days after. The little kids had to suffer all this punishment and cruelty just for the sake of a piece of dried up slab cake. This cruelty was allowed to happen, the Sisters knew what was going on but they never made any attempt to stop it. And despite all this we were still expected to go to Mass every week after we had left St John's.

To this day my mind still boggles at the sheer stupidity and cruelty of it all. I just cannot see any reason why such behaviour was allowed. Were these normal people who were in charge of us deaf children? This was a very unhealthy environment for children to grow up in. Our day was planned down to the last detail, what time to get up, what time to go to Mass, breakfast, prayers, school, dinner, play, supper, bed and we were not allowed to think for ourselves. Some boys may have liked it, but I hated every minute that I was at St Johns, the only consolation being that some of the kids became great friends. Many of them, upon reaching the leaving age of sixteen and going out into the world, were unable to cope. They were unprepared, they were institutionalised. It was a big culture shock – they were too shy or afraid to attempt to communicate with hearing people, especially women or girls. They had been brainwashed to think that it was a sin to even look at girls and the only sex education that most of us had was from one of the adult boarders, Tom Dullard. He told us not to play with ourselves or we would go blind, and if we persisted then we would get VD, which was the most terrible disease of all and the only cure was to have a red hot wire pushed up our willies, and when it was withdrawn a yellow pus came out and when that happened we were cured, but it was very painful and if no yellow pus came out of your willie then the whole process had to be repeated again – so don't play with yourself or it could happen to you!

He also told us a story about a girl who was having a bath when her pet dog jumped in with her and nine months later she gave birth to a baby that was half human and half dog. We had many such stories from this adult lodger. Can you imagine what stories like this did to little children's impressionable minds? He also told us that to become a priest one of your testicles had to be cut off so that you couldn't have an erection and didn't find women attractive any more. I used to have nightmares about it and vowed never to become a priest. Nobody was going to mess with my balls, though it was never my intention to be a priest anyway. I didn't meet a priest who was a good role model, most were too pompous and self important. It should have been their responsibility to give the children some sex education, not leave it to those stupid lodgers. I decided that I would only be interested in football and sport. There would be no girls in my life, they were too complicated. What was the point if they would lead me to sin and to suffer everlasting fire in Hell, as we were being taught. No beer or cigarettes either. I must stay fit for football. I would model myself on Stanley Matthews, Jackie

Milburn or Frank Swift. Ah well! It was almost as if we were still living in the dark ages. How could there be such ignorance in this modern age? It is a good job that none of those ridiculous lessons really sank into my mind.

Many of the leavers had been told by the teachers that their speech was very good. This was blatantly not true. It was a big shock to find out when they finally left St John's that they couldn't speak at all. They could just about recite the Lord's prayer or Hail Mary with difficulty, although many couldn't even do that. Many had difficulty trying to communicate with members of their own families, workmates or bus conductors, shop assistants etc. For many, even writing it down on paper was no use. This made many yearn to be back in St John's, not because they were happy there, but for the company of their peers and the ability to communicate with each other, which was lacking in the outside hearing world. This is the reason why such strong bonds were forged, and friendships made there often lasted for life. So began the tradition of holding Boston Spa annual reunions every year in a different British city.

Many were unable to cope with the loneliness and isolation of the outside world. The real miracle was that, despite all this, so many grew up to become normal adults. It just shows the resilience of the human spirit. What we boys had to suffer at St John's either made us strong and concentrated our inner and mental strength, or it set us on a downward spiral leading to mental breakdown or an early death. I know that I learned very early on that not all people who held positions of authority were worthy of respect and that respect had to be earned, not given just because of who or what a person is.

Could the order have been passed down from the powers that be to harden us children up by being cruel to us so that we could cope better in the harsh outside world? They were brutal times, a war was on and millions of people were being killed. Did they think that by brutalising us they were somehow fitting us for life outside the institution? I came to the conclusion that they were just sick sadists who enjoyed being cruel. Sister Margaret would sometimes leave a few coppers on the window sill in the refectory and when they disappeared we were all gathered together and given a lecture about thieves and stealing and what an evil sin it was. If nobody would confess to stealing the money, then we were all punished; maybe no sweets on Sunday or another privilege taken away. But they wouldn't dare say no to stories from Mr Caproni. I will tell you about Mr Caproni later on in my story.

When I was home for the holidays I once tried to explain what was happening at St John's to my Mam and Dad, but they didn't believe me. They said that the sisters were lovely people, and they thought that I was making it up so that I wouldn't be sent back again. Now, in retrospect, it is hard to believe that these things did happen, but you'd better believe me, they did.

The cruelty was mental as well as physical. For example, one of the boys in my class, I will call him Frank, which for obvious reasons is not his real name as he may have family still living, had a weak bladder or something wrong with him that sometimes made him wet his bed. He was picked out for an especially exquisite form of cruelty. Once when he wet his bed Sister Teresa, in her exasperation, would put these boards around his neck, front and back, written on which were the words, 'I have wet my bed again'. She would make him pick up his wet bed sheets, then she would take him over to the girls' side and parade him through all the girls' classrooms. That was the only occasion when one of the boys was allowed near the girls. Was this supposed to cure his bedwetting? I cannot imagine how this made poor Frank feel, it must have been very embarrassing for him and made him feel smaller than Tom Thumb. He must have wished the ground would open up and swallow him. He tried to run away once and he got as far as Doncaster when the police picked him up and brought him back. He had to face more punishment for running away and bringing "shame on the School". I know that when Frank left St John's he became an alcoholic and, tragically, died very young.

One day a new boy came to St John's. His name was John Dolan. He came from some tropical country, which I think was Nigeria in Africa. Anyway, we were not allowed to see him at first because, although it was spring time and we were quite warm, John couldn't stop shivering and so had to stay in bed covered with blankets and hot water bottles. Gradually John became acclimatised and was able to join us. Sister Margaret explained to us that John had come from a very hot country where there was no deaf school, so his parents had to send him to Britain to be educated. She told us that his father was a prison warder. She said this with a disdainful look at John. "A prison warden! Ugh! A prison warden! How disgusting." Luckily, John didn't understand what she was saying, so the smile never left his face. I thought that John was a very interesting lad with a brilliant sense of humour. He could waggle his ears, both together and separately, and he would do this at the most unlikely moments, such as when we were at prayers or lessons, and it was very hard not to burst out laughing. I enjoyed talking to him, but after he left St John's he stayed in England and never went back home,. Soo after he left I heard that he was in a mental hospital. I don't know if he is still alive. He is just one of many deaf people who were unprepared and so unable to cope in the hearing world.

I have often wondered why such awful people as Sister Margaret become Sisters of Charity of St Vincent de Paul. It was obviously not because she felt any pity for, or had any charitable feelings for, the deaf children. One of my friends, named Colin, told me that when his mother brought him to St John's and met Sister Margaret she was surprised because she recognised her from when she was a little girl in London many years earlier. Colin's mother said that Sister Margaret, as a girl, lived in a very poor area and was dressed in rags, so she was surprised to see her as a Sister Superior. If that was correct then Sister Margaret really had no right to have such a contemptuous attitude to the deaf children in her care. Colin also informed me that many years later, as Sister Margaret lay dying in a London Hospice, she sent for him and asked him to please ask all the boys of her time at St John's to please forgive her. So she must have known exactly what she was doing. Years later, when having a conversation with one of the lads who was older than me when at St John's, he told me that he had been bullied too, and he thought it was normal behaviour, so when he was one of the big boys he bullied the smaller boys too. I wonder if Sister Margaret was bullied and abused as a kid too.

As a child at St John's in the 1940s, I never really thought that what we children were going through at St John's was in any way unusual. I thought that it was how these religious people behaved in those sort of places. I left St John's in 1951 with a very serious inferiority complex when mixing with normal hearing people, especially women and girls. It took me many years to conquer those feelings of inferiority and shyness when dealing with hearing people. Now I think I have gone to the other extreme, I have developed a mental toughness and I think myself far superior to these hearing people who never had to go through the ordeals that my deaf childhood friends and I did.

As well as the football fields, we had a large playground, which was covered with a hard asphalt-like substance and sloped downward towards the school. Some of the boys had rollerskates and we enjoyed skating on it, especially when going down the slope. We would take turns with the rollerskates, or sometimes we would split the rollerskates up and have one each, then go whizzing down the playground balanced on one foot. Looking back, I can see that it was a very dangerous game to play, but there was no such thing as health and safety inspections in those days.

One day a lad named Terry Smith (not his real name) was whizzing down the slope at breakneck speed when something went wrong, his skate must have hit some obstruction. Anyway, he went flying through the air and landed on the asphalt with a sickening crash and knocked himself unconscious. Sister Margaret was called and she came hurrying over all flustered and red -faced to see what was wrong. When she saw Terry lying there unconscious she sent one of the boys to get Mr Young. Mr Young came and she told him to pick Terry up and take him inside. Mr Young protested that it was best to leave him there until the ambulance came. I was watching this tragedy unfolding, and I don't think that Sister Margaret had called for an ambulance. She overruled Mr Young's protests and made him pick up Terry and take him inside to the playroom, where she made Mr Young go for some water and salt. She mixed the salt in the water and forced it down Terry's throat. Terry began gagging and choking and spewed it up and Sister Margaret said, "Good! That's brought it up". I will leave you to make your own conclusion as to what she meant by that. An ambulance was then called and it took Terry to hospital.

It was several weeks before Terry came back to St John's and I was playing with some boys when he came into the playground. We rushed over to say hello to him, but when we got near to we were shocked to see that one of his arms was withered and useless, and I am sure that other boys in the play ground were shocked too. Later, Sister Margaret told us that poor Terry had caught polio and it had affected the nerves in his arm and had paralysed it, so we must pray for him. At the time I didn't know what polio was, but now I know and I very much doubt that is what happened. You cannot get polio by knocking yourself unconscious. What really happened has been hushed up. All this happened over sixty years ago and it may seem that I am raking over old coals, but it is all a part of my story so I am including it for that reason. Not long ago I met Terry at one of the annual Boston Spa reunions and when talking to him I realised that he still believes that polio had caused his left arm to wither and become useless.

Around this time I was playing football one day and was tackled from behind and fell. Putting out my right arm to soften the fall, I broke it. I was in dreadful pain. Mr Young came hurrying over and took one look at my arm and sent some boys off to get the first aid kit from the scout hut, I should mention that Mr Young was a member of the St John Ambulance Brigade and was, despite what Sister Margaret may have thought, skilled at first aid, so he made a good job of splinting and bandaging my arm. He knew that I must go to hospital and the nearest hospital was in Leeds, which was fourteen miles away. He took me to Sister Margaret and told her what had happened and asked her to get an ambulance. Sister Margaret was not taking it seriously enough for Mr Young, saying, "Oh it's not too bad is it? He will be alright tomorrow." At that Mr Young lost his patience and said in sign, "You stupid woman, this boy has broken his arm and needs to get to hospital as soon as possible." Just then Sister Teresa came to see what was happening. She weighed up the situation in a glance and hurried off to get some transport to take me to Leeds infirmary. She managed to get somebody who had a little Austin7. One of the younger Sisters, Philomena, accompanied me in it to the infirmary. There were no motorways in those days, and most of the journey was along winding, bumpy country roads. and the pain was really bad with the jolting. At Leeds infirmary we had to wait for a while, my arm was hurting and I was feeling fed up. I couldn't help having a little cry, but Sister Philomena told me to stop snivelling. I was taken into another room and given chloroform and when I woke up my arm was in plaster and my trousers were wet. We were told to come back the next day because the bones in my arm were broken in several places and they were unable to set them all properly. On the bus back to St John's, Sister Philomena was giving me disdainful looks and on arrival back at St John's she went off to give her report to Sister Margaret. I was sent to Sister Margaret's office, where I was told that I was a disgrace to St John's. I had let the school down badly with my snivelling and wetting myself and I should be ashamed of myself. A favourite saying of hers was, "Your Mother is a lady and your Father is a gentleman, but YOU! YOU! You are rubbish".

I had to make the journey to Leeds infirmary by bus every day for one week with Sister Philomena. Once there they would give me chloroform and take the plaster cast off and set the bones again, but this time I made sure that I went to the toilet first. I had a sore at the base of my thumb before I broke my arm, now with my arm encased in plaster I was unable to reach it to clean it and it started to smell. The smell steadily got worse until it was really stinking and none of the boys would sit near me. Sister Mary was in charge of the clinic, with her main duty to syringe the boys' ears out every week and look after any cuts and bruises. I had seen her about it before, but she had just told me to come back if it got worse, so I went back to see her. She said, "Ooh, that smells awful. Why didn't you come to see me sooner?" I had done so, but she had dismissed me and said come back if it gets worse. I said nothing. I had learned by then that it was a waste of time, so I just stood there looking stupid. " You silly boy, this could be really bad," she continued, and got some liquid, which I think was disinfectant. It smelled like jeyes fluid, but it was probably 'Detol'. She poured some down between my hand and the plaster, and as it hit the sore at the base of my thumb there was an explosion of intense pain. I screamed and brilliant white lights were going off inside my head. It was as if she was trying to cut my hand off with a hacksaw. I remember that I was running around in circles trying to escape from the pain. Gradually the pain subsided to a steady throb. Sister Mary then gave me an aspirin and sent me to bed.

Soon after this incident we went home for the Christmas holidays. My Mam took one look at my arm and got a whiff of the smell coming from it and took me straight to Ancoats hospital, where they cut the plaster off my arm to reveal a big lump of flesh at the base of my thumb that smelled vile. The doctors decided not to put my arm back in plaster of paris as the bones had set. They used just an ordinary elastic bandage and it was a big relief to have that heavy cast off my arm at last. They gave my Mam some ointment to put on the sore, which gradually shrunk, then disappeared. I have a scar there on the base of my thumb to this day to remind me of how incompetent and uncaring they were at St John's Institution for the Deaf and Dumb [sic] in those far off dark days of wartime Britain. I do know that it couldn't happen in today's world, maybe not because people are nicer, but because of the law that, thankfully, won't allow such things. The one positive thing to come out of this incident was that Mr Young went up in my estimation; I had more respect for him after that. Sister Teresa was a puzzle to me, though. She seemed to have a Jekyll and Hyde character.

PART FOUR

Mr Caproni and the Scout and Cub troops

NONETHELESS, ALL WAS NOT doom and gloom, so enough of this "Woe is me". We had the wolf cubs and scout troop in the evenings, with Mr Young as the cub master and Mr Caproni as the scoutmaster. Mr Young lived in a council house in the village of Boston Spa, which was about one mile away from St John's. Mr Caproni also lived in Boston Spa; he owned a row of four houses in the village. Mr Young was deaf and an ex pupil of St John's I have mentioned before in connection with punishments. Because of that, he didn't command much respect among the children. His nickname was "Foo foo" for some obscure reason. Mr Caproni, however, was different. All the boys loved him. He, too, was deaf and an ex pupil of St John's, but he had the advantage of a further private education after he left. He came back to St John's and became a teacher. He came from a wealthy family and his private education made a big difference. He was a very intelligent man. When I first entered St John's Mr Caproni was already an old man and had retired from teaching in 1933 (before I was even born). Nevertheless, he carried on teaching the boys PT and scouting.

My first impression of Mr Caproni was that he was a fierce old man with the look of an eagle with his steely gaze and his big hooked nose, and God help you if you tried to mess with him. I soon found out that he was a big softy where his boys were concerned. He always had a briar pipe in his mouth and his tweed jacket always smelled of tobacco, but it was a strangely comforting smell; it reminded me of Uncle Frank. He was a father figure to us and we just loved him. The boys of St John's couldn't have had a more perfect role model. Because he was deaf and had the ability to communicate with us on our level, we learned much more from him than from all the other teachers put together, even though he was retired and we had only a few hours with him in the evening. When he talked to us we paid attention. He gave many boys character and made us feel not so completely worthless.

One of the things he would do was keep us informed about the progress of the war. In the playroom he had erected a large blackboard and every day before prayers and school he would write on it the latest news about what was happening on the war front. Sometimes he would draw diagrams to explain it better, then he would sign it to us. And so we would follow the progress of the 8th army against Rommel in North Africa, and later through Sicily and up the leg of Italy. He also told us about the V1s and V2s on the home front (for those who don't know, these were unmanned flying bombs). His signing and body language was so dramatic, he held us spellbound. I'm sure a lot of it was from his imagination, but that is what poetic licence is all about, isn't it? If you read the newspaper reports of the war it would have seemed so dry and boring, they reported just the bare facts and dates. The way Mr Caproni told it was far more interesting; he would become the soldier as he signed and acted. For example, he would be chewing on a cigar as he kicked the door open, threw in a hand grenade, then sprayed the room with his tommy gun, leaving ten dead Nazis. When he said that we would all cheer and feel very proud to be British. That's when the sign for 'England' became the same sign that was used for friends (two hands clasped together).

We learned about the Normandy landings. We had seen all the army vehicles going past on the road outside St John's and all the aeroplanes flying over going south just before D-Day. Later he told us about the progress of the Allies closing in on Berlin as the war was coming to an end. The tension in the playroom as we were reading Mr Caproni's dramatic signing was incredible. We were five days from Berlin, then four days, then three, two, one. His signing about the British, American and Russian troops fighting street by street in the rubble and sewers of Berlin, sometimes, as it later turned out, against German boys no older than us, kept us glued there unable to move. His signing of the guns and bombs going off, buildings collapsing etc was very expressive; when you get such an expert signer as Mr Caproni words aren't necessary.

Even all the teachers, sisters and Canon Wilson himself would come to see what Mr Caproni was signing and writing on that blackboard. One day, as we were waiting for Mr Caproni to write on the blackboard, he hesitated for a long time as if he was trying to make his mind up what to write. Deep in thought, he picked up a piece of chalk and wrote just four words: 'All over, it's Peace'. The room erupted, everybody was jumping up and down cheering and hugging. We were expecting rationing to end right then and food and sweets to be plentiful. Sadly, we were to be disappointed about that.

Mr Caproni's wife wasn't deaf, so he must have been getting his information from the wireless before it was in the newspapers. Also, he was a great storyteller with a very vivid imagination, so I'm sure there was quite a bit of embellishment going on here and there to make it more interesting. Paper was in short supply so there were not as many newspapers as there are today and many people didn't know much about what was happening on the war front, but Mr Caproni's dramatic signing and little personal touches and embellishments made it far more interesting for us than the newspaper reports. Not many boys could read properly anyway. Funnily enough, they always knew what the football scores were and who played for whom. The newspapers we had to collect from the staff room we had to tear into little squares, which were hung on nails in the toilets for wiping our bums with, Now that is my definition of 'Hard Times'.

We had a massive big bonfire in the field behind the shed to celebrate the end of the war, but unfortunately sugar was still rationed so there was no toffee. In fact, if I remember correctly food was even more scarce after the war and rationing didn't end until some time in the 1950s after I had left St John's. John Dolan received a food parcel from his parents in Nigeria and in the parcel were bananas and oranges and other goodies. We all gathered around him, staring in awe at the bananas and oranges. He had a big bunch of bananas, far too many for one boy, so he teased us by telling us that bananas tasted horrible, and all the time we were all staring at him with our mouths agape and drooling. He peeled a banana, took a bite, shuddered and said, "Ugh, they are really awful," then he laughed and pulled bananas off the bunch and handed them out to us. It had been so long since we had seen bananas that some of us had forgotten that you had to peel them before you could eat them and we bit right through the peel, John had to show us how to peel them, but it didn't matter because we ate the peel anyway. We scraped the inner pith off with our teeth until the peel was paper thin, then just popped it in our mouths. I was glad that I was his friend. That was the first banana I had tasted for six years and I can assure you that not a scrap was left when I had finished with it, not even the peel.

Despite the shortage of food and, more importantly for kids, sweets, and despite the terrible environment that we were living in at St John's, it was a very interesting, exciting and historical time to be living in. As I said, I was at St John's when the war in Europe ended (V E Day) and we celebrated by having a massive bonfire and they still kept the girls and boys separated by about fifty yards on opposite sides of the bonfire. I was at home for the summer holidays when the war in Japan was brought to a close by the Americans dropping two atom bombs on the Japanese cities (V J Day). The people of Collyhurst may have been poor working class, but they certainly knew how to celebrate better than the posh people at St John's Boston Spa. On the Albert Memorial croft that was used for the wakes and fairs, they had put three army lorries together. Where they had got them from I have no idea. They piled them high with rubbish and pieces of wood that were pulled down from nearby fences and there was plenty more wood on the nearby bomb sites. All the kids had been sent to scavenge for wood, planks etc. I could see some dining room chairs on the pile and I wondered if the kid who brought them had his Mam's permission. The fence that I had tried to climb over when breaking my arm, which seemed so long ago, was ripped up and piled on top. I thought that was a fitting end for it! The whole lot was over thirty feet high and when it was set alight, flames were reached high up into the sky. People must have been saving their food rations for weeks because there were lots of spam sandwiches, home-baked cakes, sweets, and, to cap it all, crates of beer were fetched from some of the local pubs. People were really enjoying themselves, dancing and singing, as at last the war was over. Now we could get on with the business of living.

This was when I first tasted Guinness and I thought it was OK. Nobody seemed to be bothered that us kids were drinking beer. In fact, I had quite a few and ended up feeling very unsteady. Some of the older couples were creeping off into the dark corners for some hanky panky; it was a good job it wasn't at St John's or there would have been World War Three.

Back at St John's after the holidays, Sister Teresa gathered all the big boys together in the playroom and had them kneel down as she prayed and gave thanks to the Lord for sparing the world. She said that the Americans could have easily blown the world apart with their atom bombs, but the good Lord would not allow it.

As well as being a PT instructor and scoutmaster, Mr Caproni was also, as I have explained with his war stories, a skilled raconteur, with his very expressive and dramatic signing, and every Wednesday and Friday evening from 7pm to 8pm was story time, when we would sit in a semi-circle, our eyes as big as saucers, spellbound as he 'spoke' to us. His stories were not just about cowboys and Indians, though we did have a lot of westerns, especially about a hero named Jim Hatfield, but also he would sign to us about the classics too: 'The Three Musketeers, 'The Man in the Iron Mask' and other Dumas tales, 'Robinson Crusoe', 'Gulliver's Travels', 'Zorro' and many more. We would save pieces of bread from supper to eat as Mr Caproni held us, enthralled with his stories of derring do. There was a story he told us that he said was true, that it really happened. It was about meeting General Tom Thumb in London. I thought that Tom Thumb was only a fictional story but Mr Caproni said he was a real person and he had met him and had actually had a conversation with him and that he was not tiny, as small as a thumb, but about three feet tall.

There was one story that he told us that we deaf kids could relate to, though I am sure that he made it up himself. It was about a cowboy who was deaf. His moniker was 'Deaf Smith' and all the outlaws throughout the wild west were scared stiff of him. Not even Billy the Kid or Jesse James could beat him to the draw. When he took a silver dollar out of his vest pocket and started to flip it in his left hand and you could see the fingers of his right hand twitching, that was a signal to make for the hills, because Deaf Smith was beginning to lose his patience with all the skulduggery and injustice that was going on. He was always rescuing damsels in distress, and he could flip the coin and while it was still spinning in the air he could draw his gun – too fast for the eyes to follow – and shoot five baddies before he caught the coin again, dropped it in his waistcoat pocket, twirled his gun around his finger, blew the smoke away and holstered it. Deaf Smith had a special horse; its name was 'Hoss' (because that was the only word that he could actually say). Smith knew which direction danger was coming from by watching which direction Hoss's ears were turned to, so Hoss was not only his best buddy, but his ears as well. If ever he was in danger he only had to grunt "Hoss" and Hoss would come running and save him. Because they were both dumb they had a very special relationship, somewhat like a deaf Roy Rogers and Trigger. We had lots of stories about Deaf Smith and they were great stories. Mr Caproni would always stop at the most exciting part of the story... to be continued next time. "OH NO!! PLEASE!!" we would scream. "Sorry boys it's time for you to go to bed." To us kids, they were magical times.

On the Scouting side, we could beat the Navy cadets at their own game of signalling, either Morse code or semaphore, almost certainly because it was like sign language. Even though we were not allowed to leave the Institution's grounds unsupervised, Mr Caproni taught us how to find our way about, how to always know which way was north, how to light a fire. I even started to carry some pieces of tinder about with me in a watertight tin box with my jack knife, which a scout was never without, to be used in emergencies. It even had a spike for getting stones out of horse's hoofs (though I wouldn't know how to do that) and, luckily, I never got to use it for that purpose. I didn't have any matches and I never tried rubbing two sticks together, but you never knew! We were not allowed outside the school grounds unless we were accompanied by an adult, so we never had the chance to help any old ladies across the road or do bob a jobs.

Sister Teresa didn't like him teaching us how to light camp fires. She thought that boys and fires did not go well together and was a dangerous combination. We learned about knots and how to tie them, reef knots, granny knots, sheepshanks, bow lines etc. A line in the scouts creed says, "a scout is cheerful, a scout smiles and whistles", but being deaf not many of us could whistle, so I thought it was funny to see some of the boys walking about, hands in pockets, trying to look nonchalant as they blew tunelessly through their teeth. When we were in our scout uniforms we carried a staff, which was a thin pole of ash wood. On this ash pole were markings that were supposed to give you useful information, such as twelve inches to the foot, three feet to the yard etc. It had to be carried the right way up too or you were in trouble. There was also a formula using your pole whereby you could measure the height of a tree or building. I am sure that was very important information, but unfortunately I never found any use for it whatsoever.

One of the scoutmasters from Boston Spa sometimes brought his films and equipment to show us silent films about Charlie Chaplin and Buster Keaton, and we thoroughly enjoyed them. Kids were so easily pleased in those days. I was told that Mr Caproni used to be a personal friend of Lord Baden-Powell, the Chief Scout who was a veteran of the Boer war. From him Mr Caproni learned the skill of reading spoor and laying false tracks, skills which he passed on to us. I have long forgotten most of them, but at the time it enabled us to go off into a dream world of high adventure and take our minds away from our miserable existence at St John's. Maybe that was Mr Caproni's reason for teaching us all these skills. He also taught us first aid and we won the St. John Ambulance Shield a number of times. I am sure by that you can understand by now why the deaf kids adored Mr Caproni. He had lived such a full and interesting life, met many famous people, and he was showing us that our deafness need not hold us back. He was giving us confidence in ourselves and putting the idea in our minds that if he can do it, then so can we. I only understood this after I had left St John's. If ever I had a problem, I would think: 'How would Mr Caproni handle this? What would he advise me to do?'

In my time as a scout Lord Rowallan was the Chief Scout. Isn't it peculiar how the Chief Scouts were always Lords? If anybody deserved to be honoured and made a 'Sir' or 'Lord' it was Mr Caproni. He dedicated his life to teaching deaf children to be good model citizens and to live happy productive lives. He was truly the stuff that legends are made from, and as so often happens in real life, such good people are often overlooked when honours are being handed out, though I don't think Mr Caproni was at all bothered by that. He would probably have refused to accept an honour anyway. He was a modest man and not one for showy things.

****

In sport and football against the borstal boys from Thorp Arch, the Army and Navy cadets, local schools in Boston Spa, Tadcaster, Wetherby and Bramham, St John's were unbeaten, especially in the tug o' war, which was my speciality being short and stocky and strong for my age. Thanks to Mr Caproni's skills as a coach, in my years at St John's I cannot remember St John's ever losing the tug of war.

If you go through Boston Spa and cross over the River Wharfe by the bridge, you will come to the little picturesque hamlet of Thorp Arch. This hamlet boasted a tiny railway station that served Boston Spa, Clifford, St John's and the surrounding area. Just past the cenotaph, turn right and walk up the road for a few hundred yards and there on the right you will see a building with the sign 'Her Majesty's Prison'. In the 1940s that prison was the site of Thorp Arch Correction Centre, or 'Borstal' for

'Bad Boys'. We often competed with these so called 'Bad Boys' in sporting events. I remember going there once for a sporting event, racing, jumping, tug o' war etc. We were invited to dinner with them afterwards, but before the sporting event began we had to help with peeling the potatoes and shelling the peas. We had a great time, even though communication between the deaf boys and the hearing boys was difficult. The Borstal boys had difficulty understanding the strangled sounds coming from the deaf kids, but we managed somehow. The language of smiles, grins, kindness and camaraderie knows no boundaries.

Sadly, that has all vanished now; the tiny railway has long gone, courtesy of Mr Beeching. There is a lane now where the railway tracks used to run and the lovely little railway station is derelict. The Borstal is now a prison, and where there were fields there is now an industrial estate. All that I have left of those far-off balmy summer days playing with those "Bad Boys" are memories; the world has changed and moved on, and not always for the better. Ever since those days playing with the boys from Thorp Arch Borstal I seem to have had a rapport with bad lads and rebels and those who are 'Outside the Box' so to speak.

Two deaf brothers came to St John's just after the war. They came from Poland and they would gesture to us how they hated the Nazis, telling us stories about how cruel the Nazis were to the civilian people in Poland. They would point to scars on their arms and legs and indicate that German soldiers had shot them there. The scars didn't look like bullet holes to me. They were excellent athletes, far better than us. The only one who could match them in running was Colin, who was built like a greyhound, whereas I was more like a carthorse.

A boy named Jim Hathaway brought part of the Charles Atlas body building course from home. Unfortunately, it wasn't the complete course, just the part that dealt with exercises for the legs and chest, namely deep knee bends or squats for the legs and push-ups for the arms and chest. We showed it to Mr Caproni and he said it was very good, and then he told us to add another exercise, the pull-up or chin-up, to the course and do it every day. We found it very hard to do the pull-up, which we did in the doorway of the scout hut, so Mr Caproni modified that exercise and had us start the pull-up from the top by standing on a stool and lowering ourselves slowly. It worked brilliantly. Those exercises, combined with running laps around the football field in our boots, soon had us fitter than the proverbial butcher's dog. The boys soon began to show some muscular development; their legs were still skinny, but harder and faster, whereas for some inexplicable reason my legs became thicker and stronger. Mr Caproni explained to me that exercise affects people differently and we inherit a lot of our physical build from our parents, so my ancestors must have been small stocky Welshmen on my Mam's side, with some neanderthal thrown in for good measure, because my Dad was about 5 feet 9 inches and Uncles Frank and Dick were big tall men, six footers in their younger years. Even our Jimmy was tall, so I can't blame the wartime diet for being small. Anyway, I may have been small but I was perfectly formed and the girls seemed to like me as I was.

At football, Billy Jones, our centre forward, even set a record by scoring nearly sixty goals in the 1949-50 seasons, and I was selected to play for Yorkshire Schoolboys in the same season.

It must be in the dusty archives of some local newspaper in Wetherby. Billy Jones was a big lad, big-boned and massive, he was bigger than most men, so he must have been a daunting sight to the opposing team when he was heading for the goal as unstoppable as a runaway lorry full of bricks. Before we could play football on our ground we had to shoo the cows off, sometimes the big shire horses too. They left their droppings scattered all over the field and I'm sure this put many opposing teams off their game. It didn't bother us as we ran right through it, even when it was all over the ball it still didn't stop us from heading it. It also helped us with the sliding tackles, acting as a lubricant and helping us to slide further. The fact that we had cow or horse muck all over us didn't matter, winning was what mattered. We must have built up a great resistance to germs. When we were trooping off the field after a hard game of football, we were covered in mud and cow or horse muck and we couldn't get rid of the flies that were flying all round and dive-bombing us. We must have smelled just like the farm yard. We played football every afternoon, nothing was allowed to stop us playing. There was nothing more important than football, not rain and snow, hail, and fog, nothing stopped us. Our cherished football boots, which were bought by our parents, were worn out and patched up and anointed with dubbin in the cobblers shop and their life was extended far beyond what was normal for football boots. Shin pads were folded 'Beano' or 'Dandy' comics. On the really cold days our cheeks would be a bright rosy red and our noses were running like taps, our breath coming out like fog, our legs red and our fingers chapped with the cold, but all that couldn't dampen our enthusiasm.

About this time we had a new teacher. He was a big Irishman named Mr Ryan. He couldn't sign either, so there were still no teachers at St John's who could actually communicate fully with us. Mr Ryan liked to join us when we played football after dinner. He would don his shorts and rugby shirt with the green and white horizontal stripes, and while we tried to play football he would keep picking the ball up and running with it and barging us out of the way. He may have been enjoying himself, but he was spoiling our game of football, and to us that was like committing a cardinal sin. He would tell us that football was for softies and rugby was a man's game. He seemed to have forgotten that he was a big man with big bulging thighs and we were 14 or 15 year old lads. Even Billy Jones was not as big as him. This state of affairs carried on for some weeks and we were getting really fed up with him. Our football was very important to us as it was one of the few pleasures that we had and this man was spoiling it for us. Something had to be done!

One day Billy signed to me: "I've had enough of him, watch what I do to him today." The game progressed as usual, with Mr Ryan picking up the ball and drop-kicking it up the field and knocking over the boys who got in his way, until Billy and Mr Ryan were both converging on the ball and, as Mr Ryan was stooping to pick it up, Billy gave it a mighty whack and booted it right into his face from about three feet away. There were no light plastic balls in those days, this was an old leather practice ball and as the leather got old and scuffed it tended to soak up the water and become heavier and heavier as the game progressed, until it resembled a medicine ball. If you headed it correctly on your forehead as you had been taught then all was well, but if you didn't head it right it was a brain-rattling thud and it would feel like you had broken your neck and you could have a headache for the rest of the week. If the part with the leather lacing caught you on the head it could be very painful and it left a lattice mark there. Mr Ryan went over as if he had been poleaxed. It must have been like stopping a punch from Joe Louis! His glasses went flying off and ended up accidently under the boots of one of the boys and were broken beyond repair. Mr Ryan was sitting there on the grass with blood coming from his nose and looking quite dazed. He looked as if he didn't know where he was. His hand was in a cow pat too, but he was unaware of that and I'm sure that it was an unimportant detail to him just then.

So we all gathered round him and helped him up, giving him his broken glasses. Billy was profuse in his apologies and we were all saying how sorry we were. Mr Ryan never played with us again after that, even though it was an accident! Not long after this incident he left St John's. Billy Jones left St John's for good that year as well, and it would be quite a few years before I saw him again, I met him some years later at a deaf sports gathering at the White City in Manchester and I was surprised to see he had lost a lot of weight and looked very thin. I wondered if he had been ill, but I didn't like to ask. We were glad to see each other and shook hands and hugged. A year or so after that meeting I was shocked to hear that Billy had passed away. My thoughts are that better educated people have better access to the plethora of advice in books and magazines about healthy eating and lifestyles, which could have a substantial influence on the length and quality of life.

Deaf people in those days, not being able to understand the written word, didn't have that same access.

As we get older we sometimes doubt our ability to 'make a difference' in the world. I have often been asked how can we make the hearing people understand the pain the deaf have to suffer because of the ignorance and bigotry of the hearing world. Believe me, I have tried to explain but I can't. I am lucky, I have a deaf-signing background, but unlike many deaf people, and thanks to my sister Patricia, I can read and write. What I have in common with many deaf men is our expertise in turning beer and whiskey into urine. Many deaf men turned to drink to make their lives a bit more bearable. Nowadays things are slowly improving, not fast enough for me though. Sign language is being accepted and the playing field is slowly levelling out. I can only hope that I will live long enough to see deaf people really being accepted into the hearing society, and see the day when because the deaf are better educated, there will be no further need for those hearing organisations that make a profession of 'helping' the deaf.

****

When Buffalo Bill brought his Wild West Show to England in the early years of the 20th century, Mr Caproni paid him a visit and asked to be shown how to do the rope tricks that the cowboys did on the show. Mr Caproni's English was of a very high standard and so he was able to communicate through the medium of pencil and paper. Most people are basically kind and will help others less fortunate than themselves, so Mr Caproni was able to get away with more than a hearing person would, and I am sure that when he had finished telling them about his poor little deaf boys locked away in an institution far from home, he had the hardest, toughest cowpokes fighting back the lumps in their throats. Such were his powers of persuasion that he was made welcome and they showed him all the tricks of the trade. He came back to St John's with some of the special hemp ropes that were essential for the rope tricks, and very soon the boys were rope spinning as expertly as any cowboy. He also brought back some Indian clubs that he acquired from the jugglers. Even in my time at St Johns in the 1940s and '50s rope-spinning and lassooing, and swinging Indian clubs were still being taught.

Mr Caproni was a very special man and I cannot speak too highly of him. It is no wonder the boys loved him so much. He and his wife had no children of their own, but in the boys of St John's he had a massive family who loved him to bits. It was a very sad day when he died on 19th May 1949 after a short illness. He had been connected to St John's for fifty-six years, and even after his retirement as a teacher his interest and his work for the boys continued in the capacity of scoutmaster of the troop which he had formed so many years earlier. He was buried in the private cemetery behind the farm and I was honoured to be one of the escorts of the gun carriage that carried his coffin to the cemetery. He was truly a rare man. May he rest in peace.

He came to St John's to teach in 1891, eleven years after the infamous Milan Conference that banned deaf teachers and sign language in all deaf schools. Though profoundly deaf he obtained the Board of Education Teachers' Certificate. How he achieved this is a mystery, but it says much for his intelligence that he did. I have recently thought that it could have been because St John's was an institution at the time and not a school. Luckily for the boys that he taught, they were saved from a lifetime of illiteracy, unlike so many others. Most of the other teachers could, with difficulty, communicate with the hard of hearing boys, but only Mr Caproni could communicate fully with the profoundly deaf children. All through the years he was keenly interested in the boys' physical training and sports. It was also very noticeable that there were no punishments by either Mr Young or the sisters, or bullying of the small boys by the big boys, when Mr Caproni was there. I think that he was the epitome of what a deaf person could be with a good education.

He was the product of a private education, but the same standard can be achieved today with modern education if we could dispel the silly idea that BSL (British Sign Language) has its own grammar, Mr Caproni's signing followed the grammar of spoken and written English. Dear reader, if you are a hearing person please don't get upset if a deaf person says "up you" to you, I know that in the hearing world it is considered very rude, especially when accompanied with the stuck up middle finger. In deaf grammar it merely means "up to you". In the same way you hearing ladies must not get upset if a deaf man says to you that you are "well worn" for your age. He really means, in BSL parlance, that you have "worn well" for your age, so you can see that BSL users find it very hard to fit into the hearing world and can become very insular and excluded from many things, and all because of this silly idea that BSL needs its own unique grammar.

Mr. Caproni

****

After the war the food situation improved slowly. There was still rationing and we were still hungry all the time, except when a pig was slaughtered at the farm when there were sausages for breakfast on Sunday mornings. We would carry a big tin of sausages into the refectory from the kitchens and plonk it down on the serving table where the sister would serve them out. What parts of the pig went into those sausages I don't want to know, I do know that nothing was wasted, but I can truthfully say that I have never tasted such delicious sausages as those at St John's, even now, all these years after. I only need to imagine the taste and smell of them to start salivating. Today's sausages cannot compare with ours from St John's of long ago. Not a scrap was wasted, we were not used to such luxury, and when all the sausages were gone the tin was scraped clean of any traces of fat, which was spread on bread and wolfed down. We took turns on who could scrape the tin. When I come to think of it, I remember that we also scraped out the big cauldron that the porridge came in. The burnt bits at the bottom of the cauldron were the best bits and it is hard to explain their taste, but the word "nutty" comes to mind! We certainly made the kitchen staff's job of washing up easier.

At this time I had the job of washing up the crockery after meals, which I did in a room between the refectory and the kitchen. One of the cooks was a deaf lady named Edna Cooper, who took a liking to me. She called me her handsome boy and she would leave me some treats in the dumb waiter leading to the kitchen. Sometimes it would be a piece of cake or some trifle, spaghetti or macaroni cheese – not the sort of food that they were giving us. It was from the sisters' and teachers' dining room, and very rich and tasty fare it was. Do you think that nowadays, if we kept our kids on the verge of starvation then no food would be wasted? Would they clean their plates as we did, and even eat their sprouts? There would certainly not be so many obese kids around.

As you can see, our diet was slowly improving. Sometimes we had a piece of cheese with our bread at supper time and when it was in season we had rhubarb and custard every day. The rhubarb was from the extensive rhubarb beds in the vegetable garden. You may be wondering how, with the large vegetable garden and the farm, we didn't eat better. So do I! I can only surmise that the produce was being sold. Once we had some dates, which came from some place in North Africa. They came as a big compacted sand we had to cut it into pieces to share out. It was as hard as iron, but after a struggle we managed to break it up to be shared out so everybody had a piece. Another time a large tin of honey came for us from Australia, so St John's must have been known all over the world. This tin of honey proved to be impossible to open by unscrewing the cap as it was either rusted or welded on. We all tried, Mr Young, the sisters, all the big boys, none could open it. In the end the joiner, Mr Harker, had to open it with a hammer and chisel; that meant that it couldn't be sealed again, so the mice, of which there were plenty in the refectory, would get in and drown in it. Every morning the sister would fish out the dead mice before ladling a big spoonful into the porridge cauldron. Can you imagine that happening nowadays? What a furore there would be!

We still had our monthly dose of senna, even with all that rhubarb. I suppose this stopped our bowels from becoming impacted from all the stodgy food that we were given. When working in the vegetable garden we would sometimes pick sticks of rhubarb and eat them raw, no sugar. I get a shiver running up and down my spine when I think of it now. Raw sprouts, too, were popped in our mouths, and we also ate mangels, which were a type of large swede which were grown to feed the cows. They were quite nice sliced like a water melon and eaten raw. We were, I think, instinctively giving our bodies what they needed, everything helped, as we were growing lads and always hungry.

Around this time a strange thing occurred. Some new boys had come and three of them could speak. One of them was from Manchester just like me, so we had a lot in common; the other two were from York and Birmingham. Because we could speak we became friends and spent a lot of time together just talking. It felt good to speak; I had almost forgotten how to. Strangely, it seemed to infuriate Sister Teresa to see us speaking. She tried to split us up, and she said that we must not speak to each other, we must be like the other children and use sign language. I cannot explain why she said that. For the past few years I had to put up with their efforts to teach me to speak properly and lose my Manchester accent. Of course, we ignored her and continued to speak when we got together, much to Sister Teresa's chagrin. She would give us an evil look but she did nothing more about it.

The lad from Birmingham was named Kevin Price and he became a friend too. He spoke with a strong Irish brogue. One day he was teaching me to sing 'The Mountains of Mourne'. I hadn't sung any songs for a few years and it felt strange to be singing again. He had to mouth the words and sing in a loud voice for me. We noticed that Sister Margaret was taking an interest in us and coming closer to hear what we were talking about. When she was within earshot of us Kevin changed the subject abruptly and began telling me that his name was not Kevin Price, it was really Kevin O'Connor and he was proud of it. Sister Margaret's face went red with anger as she berated him: "Your name is Kevin Price, the O'Connors are murdering IRA scum and don't you forget it." She carried on ranting in a similar vein for a few minutes, then she told me to keep away from him or I would be corrupted too. I thought, 'Wow! This is interesting, it reminds me of what my Dad, Uncle Dick and Uncle Frank used to talk about in our house when they were in their cups.' Later, Kevin Price (O'Connor) told me that he wasn't deaf but had been sent to St John's to get him out of the way until some trouble had blown over. He was at St John's for two years from 1946 to 1948 and I have often wondered what became of him. He never attends the annual Boston Spa reunions. I hope that he had a peaceful life and didn't become embroiled in the troubles of Northern Ireland.

After coming back to St John's from the Christmas holidays in early January 1947, the weather turned arctic. We had snow for weeks on end. The football field was covered in three feet of snow for week after week, and the temperatures plummeted. A new ice age had begun and it was impossible to play football. It was the coldest and longest winter for many, many years. There was a large open-fronted shed at the top end of the playground, and we had invented a ball game just for in the shed. At the open end of there were some pillars holding the steel beam that supported the roof, two of which served as goalposts. The other goalposts were drawn on the brick wall opposite. The game was played inside the shed and the rules were two players for each team, the ball, which was the size of a tennis ball, had to be kicked up and rebound off the underside of the roof and, without letting it touch the floor, we had to kick it into the opponent's goal. It could become quite fast and hectic and we soon worked up a good sweat, even in winter. Some of us took our boots to the cobblers shop where we hammered some metal studs into the soles and heels so that we could skate on the ice that covered the playground. Any boy who didn't have metal studs on his boots was not allowed on our slides. We would pour buckets of water all over the playground before we went to bed and overnight it would freeze, and in the morning the playground would be a solid sheet of ice, so we had a lot of fun skating.

I forgot to mention earlier that I had a dog. Our Rusty was a brown and white mongrel that my Dad had got from the dogs' home. He was a great dog, close friend and good companion to me when I was home for the holidays. I had recently had a letter from home to tell me that our Rusty had died of old age, and because of this I was feeling very downhearted. I decided that I had enough. I was losing my patience with these crazy people, so I wrote off to the Navy Headquarters in Southampton to tell them that I wanted to join up and help to defend England against its enemies. I explained that, thanks to Mr Caproni, I was already an expert at Morse code and semaphore and I knew how to find the North Star. I thought that if I joined, I would at the same time get to see the world. I got a reply about a week later, which said thank you very much and they wished more people had the same spirit that I showed, but I was too young at thirteen years old and if I was to apply again in a few years then they would be happy to accept me. I didn't believe them, I thought that the real reason they wouldn't accept me was because of the return address that I had put on the application form, 'St John's Institution for the Deaf and Dumb'.

I was disappointed, but not beaten yet. Anyway, I only wanted to join the navy to get away from this place. After talking it over with two of the boys who could speak, Freddy from Manchester and Denvil (strange name) from York, we decided to run away, so one afternoon while we were playing in the field with the others, I gave the signal, "Are you ready?" "Yes." "Come on then!" We climbed over the gate and set off running down the road to the village of Clifford half a mile away. Someone spotted us and told Mr Young and he told some big boys to run after us and bring us back. We ran through Clifford, then Bramham and got onto the A1, which was just a little road then. We must have run for four miles before we had to stop because we were winded; we were lying there at the side of the road puffing and panting. Denvil wanted to go north, Fred and I wanted to go south and as we were arguing about it the big boys caught up with us. They were puffing and panting too and in a bad mood. I pleaded with them to let us go, but no, they wouldn't let us go. Instead, they smacked us on the head and kicked our bums and dragged us back to face more punishment from Sister Margaret's cane. We had to be severely dealt with so that other boys wouldn't get the idea that running away was easy, so in front of the whole School Mr Young gave us smacks on the back of our legs, five each leg, and Sister Margaret gave us five whacks on each hand with the cane in her office. There may be some alumni who will disagree with what I am writing, especially about the punishments, but you must realise that this is my experience of my time at St John's. The sisters and teachers had their special favourites who were never punished, so if you are one of these people then feel free to write your own story.

About this time a new sister came to St John's. She was very young and pretty. I would guess that she was eighteen or nineteen, and she told us that her name was Sister Kevin. I was puzzled about her name being Kevin; how could that be? Kevin was a boy's name. Some of the boys teased me that Kevin was a girls' name, but Sister Kevin explained to me that it was not her real name. When she became a sister she was allowed to pick another name for herself, and she liked the name of Kevin so she picked that. She pointed out that there were sisters named Sister Vincent and Sister Michael. I still thought it was strange, women having men's names, but we nevertheless became good friends. She was very different from Sisters Margaret and Teresa, most of us were in love with her.

One of the highlights of my time at St John's was the percussion band. Strange as it may seem for deaf kids to form a band, it is a fact that deaf people can feel music through the vibrations, especially of percussion instruments. Miss Holden was the teacher in class three, and she formed the percussion band and taught us how to read the music and play the instruments. A hard of hearing boy named Gerry was the conductor. Our repertoire was 'God Save The King', 'Land Of Hope And Glory', 'Londonderry Air', 'Loch Lomond' and 'Men Of Harlech'. I played the tambourine. After we'd been practising for some months, some inspectors came from the Trinity College of Music, London to inspect us, and in the intermediate Division we obtained the following report: "Total Marks 94, Honours, Ensemble etc 59 (60) Time etc. 22 (25), Conducting 13 (15)." They also stated:

This percussion band shows almost perfect ensemble and a wonderful contrast of expression. They have been excellently trained and reflect great credit on their teacher. Their time, accent and rhythm are excellent. The conductor knows exactly what to do and what to expect. A very great pleasure to hear a band so well trained and so efficient.

Praise indeed! We were very proud of that report and went about our daily chores with a feeling of exhilaration for some time after, and the drummer, a boy named George, went about with two drum sticks drumming on everything, even on some of the little boys' heads. We had achieved something; we didn't feel so worthless.

So there were good times as well as the bad times, but even the good times could not make up for the separation from our families that we had to endure. I missed my Mam and Dad, our Jimmy and Pat badly. Some of the boys told me that when they went home for the holidays they felt like strangers to their own families and the alienation was getting worse every year.

For some deaf children, when it came time for them to leave St John's at the age of sixteen they found that their families didn't want them. They had got used to not having them at home and couldn't face the responsibility and the communication problems of having a deaf child living with them. Some deaf kids found that their siblings resented having to share the home with them. Of course, not all families were like that; it only seemed to happen to the profoundly deaf children, not the hard of hearing children whose communication problem wasn't as bad. The kitchen staff and servants at St John's were mostly deaf people who were not wanted by their families. Many of the girls had it very bad when they left and many of them told me years later when we met that they were sexually abused by members of their families because they couldn't hear or speak. The percentage of sexually abused deaf children was far higher than 'ordinary' children.

Tom Dullard, whom I have mentioned before in connection with our sex education or lack of it, was one of these unwanted children and lodged at the Institution. He worked for a local builder. Another lodger was 'Old Joe', who was in his eighties when I was at St John's and he had been there since he was eleven, so he must hold the record for the longest residency at St John's. Strangely, I can find no mention of him anywhere in the school reports, nor can I find any photographs of him. It's as if he never existed. He was a harmless old man who had never grown up intellectually. Old Joe wasn't deaf, he could hear perfectly, but he wasn't right in his head, he was very simple-minded and he used to wander around amongst the children singing, 'Oh me Darlin; Oh me Darlin; Oh me

Darlin Clementine!' or 'God save the King'. He came from a very wealthy family of coal merchants from Merseyside; amongst others they supplied coal to the White Star Company of Titanic fame, so a lot of their coal must be at the bottom of the Atlantic Ocean now. Poor 'Old Joe', he must have been an embarrassment to his wealthy genteel family, so they paid for him to be kept in St John's for the rest of his days. He's buried in the private cemetery at the farm.

Another old man buried there is Henry Dunn. I don't know much about his history, only that he scared the little children when he went through their dormitory on his way to the toilet at night. He had a very red, bulbous, pock-marked nose that looked as if it had been stung by wasps. He also had a long white beard, was dressed in a long night gown and had a sleeping cap on his head. He carried a lighted candle and seemed to float like a ghost through the darkened dormitory, just like someone from a Charles Dickens story. We would be peeking over our blankets, eyes as big as saucers, as he passed by. He died when I was nine years old and we all had to walk past his open coffin and look at his body, which was really scary.

How many others with similar stories to tell had there been over the years? There are quite a few graves of deaf people in the graveyard of St Edward's in the nearby village of Clifford, some of them children who had died while at St John's, others deaf people who had left St John's but couldn't fit in in the hearing world and had fond memories of when they had friends with whom they could communicate fully, unlike in the hearing world, and so wished to be buried near St John's when they died. I think that this situation could only have come about because St John's was an 'Institution', not a school, and so we were placed there under false pretences. Our parents had been informed that it was a 'School for the Deaf', when in realty it was an 'Institution for the Deaf and Dumb'. We were never schoolchildren, we were inmates, and a look at the census reports will, I'm sure, bear this out. We were the children that the education authorities had forgotten about, or didn't know what to do with. Truly we were the forgotten children.

Another new teacher for class five (which was the highest class) who arrived after the war was Mr Taylor, and he couldn't sign either, so he couldn't really communicate with the other children. But I had no problem understanding him. I had hearing and speech up until I was seven, and that made a big difference, so I had an unfair advantage over the other boys. Most of the teachers took the easy way out and concentrated on the hard of hearing kids who were easier to teach, but Mr Taylor really tried to teach all the kids. If he had been allowed to learn sign language and communicate with the kids through that medium, I am sure he would have been a great teacher.

Mr Taylor looked like Hitler, he had the same hairstyle and facial features, only the moustache was missing. The other boys in the class didn't like him. They were saying that he really was Hitler and he was only pretending to be a teacher so that the British army couldn't find him. This dislike of him stemmed from the fact that they were unable to understand what he was saying as he was not an easy person to lip read. I thought he was alright, he tried to teach us English not German and get us interested in reading, and get us to join the library in the village. The other boys didn't understand written English; they had never been taught English. The attempts of the teachers to teach English to the deaf children had failed miserably because they were not allowed to use sign language. He tried to teach them lip reading, but they didn't like that. Lip reading is a myth anyway. If you were born with the ability to hear you can call on your memory of what sound was like, and that is a tremendous help. It's very difficult to learn if you are born deaf. He would spend an inordinately long time teaching lip reading at the expense of other educational subjects. They just wanted to use their own language, which was signing, that would enable them to get their brains working, not just try to recite words parrot-fashion. It was yet another example of how the teachers were already handicapped before they even began to teach because of the communication problem and not being allowed to use sign language.

I think that the kids missed Mr Caproni and his stories badly. Thanks to our Patricia I had kept up with my reading when at home during the holidays and so I was the only one interested in joining the library at first, then later two other boys, Peter and Colin, showed an interest as I got them to read the captions on the comics instead of just looking at the pictures. So Mr Taylor would take us to the library once a week and I would have two books to take out. Some of the boys thought that I was strange because of that and called me a creep behind my back, but I didn't care; a few well-placed kicks on the football field soon stopped that! I was becoming a book worm; I was only interested in playing football, reading and working in the vegetable garden. I found that working in the vegetable garden, away from the insanity in the institution, gave me an inner calm. Maybe it was something in the soil, I loved getting soil on my hands. The farm, vegetable garden and fruit orchard at St John's was fully organic, there were no garden centres in those days. The vegetables and fruit trees were fed nothing but manure from the farm, as far as I can remember the only chemical we used was lime. Seeds and cuttings were saved by ourselves from the vegetables and other things. Mr Shann taught us all this and even now I have an allotment and grow all my family's vegetables following Mr Shanns methods. I find it very relaxing working on the allotment. Maybe it was being close to nature, watching the seasons come and go and the cycle of birth, growth and death. I think that nowadays too many people are separate from nature; they are no longer whole. It's some kind of miracle if they're not insane, or maybe they secretly are. They move from office to car and then on through the traffic jams on the overcrowded roads to their suburban homes, they stress out constantly, they lose sleep, they eat badly; they are living as far from how nature intended as you can get. It's no wonder obesity and heart attacks are so prevalent.

By now I would be fourteen years old and I had learned to accept what was happening to me in this strange place. I was too big for the bullies now, they had moved on to easier targets. I had learned to go with the flow and ignore the strange (to me) people who ran the place. By now my friends, Denvil, Freddie, Kevin Price (O'Connor), etc. had all left. I played football, read my books (a favourite was O'Henry) and counted the days to when I would be leaving that place for good: Two more years, 365 days x 2 = 730 days. Oh no! 730 days! No! I can't do it, I'll go stir crazy and I'll be a gibbering wreck. Wait a minute, what about the holidays. Is that two summer holidays and two Christmas holidays? Never mind, subtract them anyway, ask Cyril to help. Cyril said six weeks Summer holidays is 6 x 7 = 42, so double that and you get 84. Then three weeks Christmas holidays is 3 x 7 = 21. Double that and you get 42, so add 84 and 42 = 126. Take away 126 from 730 = 604 days until I leave. Cyril did this in a flash, he didn't need pencil and paper, but it was still a long time! I told myself to try to forget about it, just grit your teeth and plod on and the time will soon pass. Anyway, why would I want to change this beautiful countryside for the grime of Collyhurst. Deep down I knew that I was kidding myself, the time was going to drag on interminably, and the nearer I got to leaving time the longer it would seem.

Sometime about then the Bishop of Leeds decided to send a young priest to assist Canon Wilson in the running of St John's. Father Ronchetti was the name of this young priest. He was dark and very Italian-looking, and very gentle. I took a liking to him immediately. He didn't try to force his views on us as the other adults did, he loved cricket and he would play with us nearly every day in the summer. He gave us many tips on how to put spin on the ball when bowling, how to bowl a googly and how to keep a straight bat when batting, and my batting and bowling improved thanks to him. He had a small car and he would take four boys at a time out for a drive to York, Leeds or Harrogate. The taste of freedom, just to get away from the school environs, if only for a short time, was great. Things were really getting better, the bad old days of cruelty and bullying seemed to be receding. He took me to Leeds to a sports shop to buy some cricket gear, bats, balls, leg guards, gloves etc., and while we were there we went to the pictures. I can't remember what film was showing, maybe it was 'The Song of Bernadette' or some such film, but I can remember that on British Movietone News it was showing the British middleweight champion Randolph Turpin beating the American champion Sugar Ray Robinson to become the middleweight champion of the world. Father Ronchetti must have seen how interested I was in the boxing because a few days later a set of boxing gloves mysteriously appeared in the scout hut and Cyril and I used them to spar with each other. Cyril was a bigger lad than me and he had a longer reach, and if I punched him hard he would start pummelling me and knocking me all over the place. He gave me a bloody nose once, so I stopped sparring with him and looked for someone smaller, but no one else was interested in boxing. We really needed someone who could teach us how to box and I don't think Father Ronchetti knew enough about it to be able to teach us. Maybe Sister Margaret could!!

PART FIVE

Leaving St. John's

AS THE TIME FOR MY leaving St John's was getting nearer and nearer, so I was getting more and more excited, and I am sure the same was happening with the other boys who were leaving with me. For the past few weeks we had been making our going home suits under the tutelage of the tailor, Mr Beercock. I was making myself a double-breasted pinstripe suit with wide padded shoulders, like the one that the gangsters such as George Raft wore in the films. Sadly, the whole tough guy effect was to be spoiled because we had to wear a label in the button hole with our names and addresses on in case we wandered off and got lost.

Sister Margaret told us that Father Ronchetti was going to have a talk with all us senior boys in class five on Wednesday and we couldn't contain our excitement trying to guess what this talk would be about. Colin said that because of our ages we were old enough to be told about sex and how to make love to girls and give them babies and that is what the talk was to be about, to make us ready for marriage when we left St John's the next summer. Colin also said that he already knew how to make babies, you just put your willie in the girl's belly button and that's how you made babies. His sister had told him all about it. This sort of talk got the testosterone bubbling up inside us and we couldn't wait for Wednesday to come because what Colin said made sense.

On Wednesday morning Father Ronchetti entered our classroom and asked Sister Margaret to leave. She must have had the same thoughts as us because I could see that she was reluctant to leave the classroom. We were agog with excitement and Colin kept digging me in my ribs with his elbow and rubbing his hands. Father Ronchetti couldn't sign, so we had to try to lip read him, so we were never really sure that we understood what he was saying. Cyril signed to me, "He will have to draw pictures of women on the black board for us." We were all holding our breath waiting for him to begin. Finally, he began his talk. This is the gist of what I could understand. He said, "Children, you will soon be leaving school and going out into the world. It's a very wicked world and many people will try to corrupt you, but if you go to Mass and confession every week then you will be safe. If you miss Mass then you must go to confession as soon as possible after, so that you can be forgiven. You cannot go to Heaven unless you are sorry and confess your sin, but you must try your hardest to go every week. The very, very least you must do is your Easter duty." He carried on in a similar vein about us meeting bad women whom we must avoid, never put your arms around them or become too familiar with them, especially if they are not Catholic, or they will lead us astray. By now we were all looking at each other with disappointment on our faces. He was telling us to avoid the sort of women that we were all hoping to meet when we left St John's – and we wanted to meet women who were the exact opposite of Sister's Margaret and Teresa!

At the end of his talk, Father Ronchetti gave us each a small crucifix and a small book entitled, 'Faith and Love through Christ'. I noticed that the author was Rev. WJ Hayward, who was the same priest that I had been advised to avoid by Sister Teresa. It was all very confusing. Father Ronchetti made the sign of the cross over us and said, "May the Lord guard you and guide you always. God bless you all."

What a let down that talk with Father Ronchetti was! I think that he had the responsibility to give us some sex education before we left St John's and he was shirking that responsibility, or maybe he knew as little about sex as we did. He never asked us if we had any questions for him, but we had lots of questions we would have liked to ask but never got the chance to do so. We would have to learn about sex the hard way when we left! Is there a hard way? He could have given that talk to the little kids in class one or two. Were there no teachers capable of reaching into the minds of we deaf children and putting knowledge and learning there. Certainly we were eager to soak up all the knowledge that we could and learn all that we could that would fit us for life outside the Institute. None of the teachers at the time were capable of doing that. They couldn't see the potential that many of the boys had, and I am sure that many of the girls had too. I wonder if they really understood the serious harm they were doing to the minds of these deaf children. They were setting limits when they should have been encouraging us to reach for the sky. It seemed to us that they had given up on us having a good life in this world and so were preparing us for Heaven, where we would have a better life. So we were leaving St John's full of doubts and insecurities, with no self esteem or confidence and afraid to even look at women or girls. Until Canon Kelly came along and changed all that. When I have visited the place I cannot help noticing what a difference there is in the deaf children there compared with the children from my era. Their language, demeanour and confidence is outstanding. The big difference between today's deaf kids and deaf kids of my era is today's deaf kids all seem to have either a hearing aid or cochlear implant, which were lacking in the old days. I am sure that must help them enormously.

****

I left St Johns for the last time at the age of 16 in the summer of 1951, in July to be exact. Leaving with me were Colin, Cyril, Willie Kelly and Tony Vaux. We were full of excitement and apprehension thinking what the future had in store for us. It was very hard to contain our excitement. We were really going into the unknown because at St John's in those days there was no career officer to advise us about jobs, we had no jobs waiting for us when we got home, and we had no qualifications of any kind whatsoever. We were completely unprepared to face the complexities of working in the hearing world. I wondered how many deaf kids had over the years been institutionalised and then, after becoming completely dependent on hearing people, were turned out into the hearing world that they had been kept away from for so long. How on earth were they expected to cope? Ever since the 1880s, when sign language was banned and the oral method was made compulsory, deaf kids had not stood a chance of making it in the outside world.

Sitting here today and looking back over the years that have passed all too quickly, it seems incredible that on reaching the age of 16 the authorities could wash their hands of deaf kids just like that. It was going to be hard for us to find a good job, or any job. There was no equal opportunities commission to make sure that we were not discriminated against in the job stakes. Doesn't it make your mind boggle? But we were not thinking about anything like that just then; getting a job was the last thing on our minds. Far more important, and just beginning to sink in, was the realisation that we would not be going back to St John's ever again. We were just starting to get a taste of that heady sense of freedom.

Here we were, at Leeds railway station waiting for the trains that would take us away from here. Willie, who came from Liverpool, would be travelling on the same train as me. When I got off at Manchester he would continue on to Liverpool. Colin from London and Tony from Birmingham would be travelling together. Cyril, who came from Maryport in Cumberland, had different travelling arrangements.

We kept apart from the other kids who were not leaving. We were not like them, we were different, we were men of the world. We felt really sophisticated and grown up in our pin-striped double-breasted suits. I had made my suit myself in the tailor's shop at St John's under the tutelage of Mr Beercock. I asked myself, was it worth having my bum covered in holes from his needle? I decided, yes! I'll forgive him. I would like to think that all the talk of hating the Irish was just that, talk. My trousers were held up by braces because Mr Beercock had advised that a belt would spoil the hang of the trousers. Now the lapels on the coat were beginning to curl down and would need pressing again when I got home. My socks were held up by suspenders that went round my calves. It sounds silly now but in those days it was 'cool' and I felt very suave. That morning before we left St John's, Sister Teresa made us tie labels with our names and addresses on. She said that it was in case we got lost. Now we took the labels off and threw them away. We were not kids any more. The sister who was there to make sure that we got on the right train had the good sense to say nothing. She may have known that we were really scared and full of apprehension about what the future held for us and that we were acting with bravado to hide those negative feelings. A few of the smaller kids who were not leaving tried to copy us and throw their labels away, but we made them put them back on and told them that when they were 16 and proper grown up men like us then they could throw their labels away, but not until then.

Feeling very daring, I took out a pack of woodbines and offered them around. Well, we were not kids any more and to all intents and purposes we were grown ups and men of the world. Willie took one and flipped it up and caught it in his mouth, just like he had seen Jimmy Cagney do in a film. He caught it on his third attempt. We lit up and I suppressed a cough as the smoke hit the back of my throat. We shook hands and promised to keep in touch and never to forget each other. Willie, who looked like a very young Mickey Rooney, said, "I saw a fish and chip shop outside the station, let's go and buy some." We all agreed that it was a good idea, so we threw our cigarettes away (thankfully), also our packed sandwiches, which went into the rubbish bin, and we trooped outside to the fish and chip shop. I was elected the spokesman as I was the best speaker. In fact, I was the only one able to speak, after a fashion.

I approached the shop assistant nervously and said, "Fish, chips and mushy peas five times please" as casually as I could, hoping that I had said it right. The assistant didn't bat an eyelid, she just served us with a cool expression as if nothing extraordinary was happening. Little did she know that we had just that day been released from an institution for the deaf and dumb after serving sentences varying from eight to ten years. The others looked at me in admiration and, indeed, it was a big step that I had just taken. Willie said, "Did you see that? Kev looked just like Alan Ladd when he spoke then. I wish I could do that." We paid our shilling each, laced our portions with a generous helping of salt and vinegar and went back into the station, eating them out of the newspaper wrapping. I thought, 'This feeling of freedom is wonderful, and these fish and chips are good too.' Don't forget that our conversations are in sign language, though I can't remember if my thoughts were in sign language too.

It was time for Willie and I to board our train, so we shook hands with Colin, Tony and Cyril and vowed again to never lose touch with each other. There was a lot of soot flying about from the train and some of it was going into our eyes, so it looked as if we were crying, but we weren't really, perish the thought. Willie Kelly, though he was only a little lad, was a great footballer. He was best friends with Billy Jones, another Liverpool lad whom I have mentioned before. Billy had left St John's the previous year and Willie was looking forward to meeting up with him again in Liverpool. Despite his small stature, it sometimes seemed that Willie was made from barbed wire and broken glass, he was so tough. All the knocks and kicks that he gets on the football field didn't seem to affect him, he could give as good as he got. I have seen him knock down players twice his size, and when the referee isn't looking I have even seen him... whoops! Say no more, Kev. Years later, Nobby

Stiles of Manchester United seemed to have modelled himself on our Willie Kelly.

The train taking us home from St John's for the last time set up a rhythmic tick-tack clacking as it sped us on our way home. D-dum D-dum... D-dum D-dum... D-dum D-dum; the vibrations as the wheels went over the joins in the rails travelled right up our legs. Willie and I talked about his plans now that we were free. I had no plans at all, I was just going to go with the flow and let the fates decide. Willie had a far away look in his eyes as he told me of his plans to join the Liverpool deaf clubs football team and join up with Billy Jones, who was already playing for them. After that he said that they (Billy and him) might join Liverpool football club as professionals and play with Billy Liddell. That was as far ahead as he could think for the moment. In fact, football was all these Liverpool lads seem to think about.

The train finally pulled into Manchester's Exchange station. With a last handshake and promise to keep in touch with Willie, I stepped off the train clutching my small suitcase. I was almost knocked over by our Patricia, who ran at me and jumped into my arms, and then our Jimmy and Mam appeared. We just stood there having a group hug for some minutes. When we finally pulled apart, we looked at each other. Mam said, "Kevin, you have grown since Christmas, there'll be no more going back to that place now." Pat said, "Kev! You look so brown, wait until my friends see you, you look like Larry Parks." Who was Larry Parks? And Jimmy said, "Kev, I've talked to my boss and there's a job for you as an apprentice cabinet maker when you're ready." I was too overcome with emotion to say anything. I remember

I just stood there looking at their pale city complexions and thinking, 'This is wonderful, home for good at last, this is great, thank you God.' This was a new beginning. I was about to get on with the rest of my life, ready to face any challenge. I had a great feeling of euphoria because I had finally left that horrible place, though I would dearly miss the friends that I had made there.

We walked out of the railway station and made our way to Cannon Street Bus Station, and on the way I could see big gaps in the buildings where the German bombs had flattened them. There were bomb sites all over Manchester, it was very bleak and dismal-looking after the clean countryside of Boston Spa. Nevertheless, I was glad to be home again. We got on the trolley bus, which took us up Rochdale Road to Churnet Street, where we alighted for the short walk up Churnet Street to our house. We passed the Acme Tin Stamping Company, which now had a new roof after the old one had been burnt off during the war. We also passed the Civic Hall, where we used to have those dreadful school dinners so many years ago.

A conglomeration of memories were flooding through my head as we entered the door of 40 Northern Drive. Nothing much had changed, there was the cast iron coal-fuelled fireplace with the swivelling hobs that kept the kettle on the boil. I thought, 'Oh, gosh! I'll have to share the bed with Jimmy again, no more sleeping in my own bed.' Can you see the way I was thinking differently after all those years at St John's, 'Oh, Gosh!' instead of 'Bloody 'ell!. I found it quite difficult to adjust to the hearing world again; I had to consciously stop myself from signing when talking to Mam, Jimmy or our Pat, and some of the neighbourhood kids would laugh at the way I pronounced some words.

My sister Patricia, though only 14 at the time, decided to take me in hand and teach me to pronounce words correctly. The English language can be very confusing if you cannot hear it spoken. It is not a phonetic language, many words are not pronounced the way you would think they should be because of the way they are spelled. An example is Blackley, which is a Manchester district to the north of Collyhurst. It is spoken as 'Blakely'. Another is Bury, spoken as 'Berry'. Words ending with 'ue', such as tongue or league, are very confusing to deaf people. They aren't pronounced 'tongoo' or 'leagoo', as a deaf person would expect. Thank God we don't live in Wales! I got lost in Wales once and found it impossible to ask directions. I just couldn't say the words right. There were many words that confused me, and many people tend to stretch out their sentences with unnecessary words. Even today lots of people say things like, "at this moment in time" instead of just saying "now", or "at the end of the day". I'm not sure what that's supposed to mean, but it's all extra work when you're trying to lip read them. Funnily enough, I could say my prayers and pronounce the words perfectly. And so could many of the boys from St John's, because we'd been taught how in our speech lessons by the sisters. But after a few years in the hearing world that changed; they could then pronounce many swear words perfectly. I am sure that many of the people that I came into contact with and tried to talk to thought that I was a foreigner because of the way I spoke. Sometimes they would ask me to repeat what I had said. They would be giggling and sniggering and calling to their mates to come and listen to this strange kid; their ignorance of what being deaf meant was staggering to me.

After being in an institution for the deaf and dumb for eight years and using sign language as my main means of communication, I had to learn how to speak all over again, so altogether it was quite a daunting prospect that I faced. Without my sister Pat I would have found it very hard indeed. The one positive thing that being deaf and the butt of hearing people's jokes was that it had given me an inner strength and a steely resolve to make it in the hearing world. Remember, this was in the years before the small, behind the ear hearing aids; very few deaf people wore hearing aids then. I have always thought of myself as being deaf, not hard of hearing. I couldn't use a phone and even today with my behind the ear digital hearing aid I still can't use a phone.

The massive hearing aid that I was given as a kid was dug up from somewhere by our Pat and she told me that I must wear it when she was giving me speaking lessons because every little helped. She was becoming quite a little bossy boots. I knew that she was doing it because I was her brother and I really wouldn't be able to make it in the hearing world without her help, and I was very grateful to her and thought that she would make a brilliant teacher. I didn't mind wearing that cumbersome hearing aid for the speech lessons, but only for the speech lessons. It did help me to get the sound of the words right, but it was a relief to get it off again afterwards and go back into my soundless world, which was far more peaceful and relaxing. That hearing aid was far too unwieldy and cumbersome to wear all the time. I could only hear certain noises with it and I couldn't distinguish any words, besides, I was already a figure of fun to most of the local kids and I didn't want to make it worse.

Our Pat would go with her friends to Finnegan's Dancing Academy on Queens Road and she wanted me to go with them to learn to dance. She thought that it would help me with my speech. Maybe she thought talking to her friends would help me to overcome my shyness with girls; maybe she was being a matchmaker, trying to get me a date with one of her friends, but I refused to go. I was far too shy and uneasy in the presence of girls, thanks to Sister Margaret and Sister Teresa. Maybe I should have gone, but memories of Miss Harker and her dreaded Morris dancing and her cane on my legs exhorting me to lift them higher and higher came back to haunt me and put me off dancing.

I often wondered how Colin, Cyril, Willie and Tony were managing. If I was finding it quite hard to adjust to the hearing world, it must have been a lot harder for them. I had kept in touch with Colin and we would write each other letters now and again, but it would be useless to ask how they were getting on because I knew that pride would never allow them to admit it if they were finding it hard going. I knew that this was where the Walter Mitty complex took over. They would never be just a tailor, oh no! They would be bespoke tailors on Saville Row making suits for Winston Churchill and film stars; never just a gardener, but a 'landscape expert', or instead of a carpenter they would be an 'antique furniture restorer'. Surely they are allowed to have a bit of pride.

After lazing about getting my bearings for a couple of weeks, I started work as an apprentice cabinet maker. Jimmy took me one morning and introduced me to his boss and workmates and I was able to start work there and then. The furniture factory was situated in an old mill on Pollard Street in Ancoats. Every morning we would walk the two miles through the mean streets of two up two down grimy terraced houses and across the bomb sites. Many of the people kept dogs and others kept pigeons in coops on top of the outside loo, so we had to be careful where we put our feet.

My job at the furniture factory consisted of gluing wooden reinforcing blocks to the legs and sides of small coffee tables to stiffen them up. There were hundreds, nay thousands, of them, all piled up behind me. I would pick one up, turn it over, stick two blocks of wood to each leg, then put it in a pile in front of me. After two weeks of doing this I was bored to distraction. I thought that this wasn't cabinet making; in fact, I hadn't seen one handsaw or chisel or any other wood working tool, it was all done by machines. There was no skill involved at all. It was completely different from the way I had been taught by Mr Harker in the carpentry shop at St John's.

One day, being thoroughly fed up and bored out of my mind, I plucked up the courage to approach the foreman and ask him for a change of job. At first he didn't seem to understand what I was saying. I thought that my speech was good, what was he playing at? I finally made him understand what I wanted. He told me not to worry, there would be a change next week when I would be gluing the blocks on the legs of dining room chairs as there was an order for thousands of them.

By now I had lost my healthy rosy-cheeked look and had a pale city complexion. I was doing the most boring job in the world and all for the princely sum of two pounds ten shillings a week. Cor! What a lucky lad I was. At first I didn't understand what was going on, then slowly it dawned on me that they were thinking that because I was deaf I was incapable of doing other jobs, and gluing table and chair legs was all that I could do and I should be thankful that they were allowing me do that. Remember, at St John's we had been told to be good workers and to know our place in the hierarchy of society. I was finding out that meant right at the very bottom.

Most of the deaf lads from St Johns left at sixteen with massive inferiority complexes, which was a result of the terrible education that we had been given. I know that I did, and it would be quite a long time in the future before I realised that I was a far superior person intellectually than the average hearing person. Even though they had been told that I was deaf, I was continually being asked stupid questions such as, who did I like best Nat King Cole or Al Martino? I had to read up on them to find out who they were. That's when I found an article about Johnny Ray, a singer who was hard of hearing and wore a hearing aid. Not one like mine, of course, it was a small invisible one, very expensive. So next time I was asked that question I said "Johnny Ray", even though I had never heard any of them sing and wouldn't do so until well into the future when digital hearing aids and neck loops were available. Even then I had to know the lyrics before I could follow the song.

I was missing the green countryside of Boston Spa and working in the vegetable garden, my deaf friends and the easy carefree way that we would converse in sign language. I was thinking, 'Come back Sister Margaret, come back Sister Teresa. I didn't really mean those nasty things that I said about you before.' I would have gladly put up with them, if only I could have a nice relaxing conversation in sign language with my deaf friends, just once more. It was so stressful trying to make it in the hearing world, where I had to crane my neck forward and strain my eyes trying to follow conversations. Lots of people looked on me as being strange and weird because of the way I spoke, and many times we would be talking at cross purposes because they had changed the subject of discussion without letting me know. They didn't like it if I asked them to repeat what they had said. When I asked them, they would say, "Never mind, doesn't matter" or "Forget it", and they would roll their eyes heavenwards and shake their heads as if I was stupid for not understanding them, anything rather than bring me into the conversation and repeat what I had missed. I am sure there are many deaf people who can empathise with what I am saying. Without the help and support of our Pat I would have given up in despair. I decided then that I couldn't carry on like this, I must do something.

Once again I approached the foreman and, after some difficulty, I managed to make him understand that I wanted a change of job. He said that he would see what he could do; he had shifty eyes and I could see that he didn't really mean it.

What was wrong with my speech? I had always assumed that I could speak well, apart from mispronouncing difficult words. I could control the volume of my voice thanks to Miss Harker. My English was good, and thanks to our Pat's encouragement I could read and write better than many of these hearing people. Was my speech really so bad? Lots of people had no difficulty understanding me. Was this shifty-eyed foreman pretending not to understand me so that he could use it as an excuse to keep me doing these menial jobs? I was beginning to doubt myself and to lose what little self confidence I had. I had no qualifications at all, except for a certificate to show that I had passed an exam in religious knowledge. I knew that to get anywhere I must get some qualifications. I didn't want to work in an office, I enjoyed using my hands and I didn't mind getting them dirty.

One day I read in the newspaper that there were places for students in the technical college in Greenheys, which was across town, so I went one day after work to enrol. After explaining that I was deaf and the reason why I had no qualifications, I was told that it would be impossible for me to enrol on any of their courses. The reason given was that I would hold the other students back and it wouldn't be fair to them. I tried some other colleges with the same results. Isn't that amazing? It seemed that the people who needed help the most didn't get it; instead they got a kick in the bum. Criminals and drug addicts were treated better. I was finding out what discrimination by bigots was all about. What made it worse was that these people were the educated ones, but, hey, I should have known that from my experiences at St John's. It would be many years in the future before the Equal Opportunities Law made it illegal to discriminate, and at first it was only for the benefit of immigrants, not for people with disabilities. Land of Hope and Glory! Yeah, right. Today many employers and other people in authority only pay lip service to the Disability Discrimination

Act (DDA). There are too many loopholes they can use to get round it.

I approached my speech lessons with our Pat with a renewed vigour. Dammit! I was going to show them they can't dismiss me just like that. After some months of Pat's coaching, and by focusing fiercely, my speech was improving. It was much better now and I was very grateful to her and I loved her to bits. Anybody who messed with our Pat would have me to deal with. Pat was being educated by the sisters in St Joseph's convent. She had won an eleven plus scholarship to be able to go there. Our Pat was a very clever girl and very mature for her age. I think this convent was somewhere in Levenshulme, which was a district across town. According to Pat these sisters were very different from the ones at Boston Spa. Her sisters were very kind and thoughtful and excellent teachers. Cynic that I was becoming, I wondered if it was because Pat came home every day, unlike us kids at Boston Spa who were kept behind locked doors.

I remembered Mr Caproni and the way he would train us for sports. He was very innovative and he was always coming up with fresh ideas. I remembered that he had given us some advice one day about the Charles Atlas course, so I sent off for the full course one day. Grrr! Nobody was going to mess with me, right? The first part of the course arrived a week or so later, and so, without further ado, I got stuck into it. All that excess energy that had been building up in me since leaving St John's went into those exercises, squats, push ups, pull ups, sit ups, etc. I put everything I had into them and I immediately began to feel better. These exercises got rid of a lot of the aggression that had been building up inside me because of people's attitudes towards me. Whether real or perceived it didn't matter, I seemed to be on the defensive all the time in the hearing world. I was never like this when I was with my deaf friends.

The Charles Atlas course built up my bodily strength. I put everything I had into those exercises, I squatted and did push up until the sweat poured off me and gathered in puddles on the floor around me, and I could feel myself getting calmer as the days passed. I'm sure that but for Mr Atlas I would have ended up in trouble with the police. I also went to the YMCA gym in Peter Street, Manchester, where I learned to box and how to punch my weight, and also how to ride punches. I also joined the wrestling team. I thought that because of the way things were going for me in the hearing world that knowledge and ability would come in handy one day. I must have had a lot of aggression inside me that needed to come out as it felt good to get stuck in and work up a sweat. After showering and going home on the bus I felt all pumped up and invincible. Bring 'em on!

Another instalment of the course arrived one day; this one was dealing with nutrition. Fresh air and water were very important elements in a healthy life. Mr Atlas advised eating lots of steak and drinking gallons of milk. He probably didn't know that we still had rationing here in Britain. He also advised exercising in front of an open window first thing in the morning and bathing your vitals in ice water. He also advised keeping a glass of water with some nails in it and taking a drink of it every day and keeping it topped up, to put iron into the body to make us strong. He said that these were the secrets of the olde tyme strong men, and in imparting these secrets to me, he was giving me very valuable advice that some people would pay hundreds of dollars for. But I won't charge you anything for telling you these secrets, he explained.

Next morning, bright and early, I jumped out of bed, threw open the window and started on my squats. The east wind from Siberia blowing over the Pennines into our bedroom sent the curtains billowing with their icy blast and Jimmy, who was huddled under the blankets, shouted, "Kev! Kev! Shut the bloody window, it's free-ee-zing!" I quickly shut the window and decided that Mr Atlas lived in some tropical place, maybe Florida, because in a previous lesson he had advised that muscles must be kept warm when exercising them.

I asked Jimmy, "What are your vitals Jimmy?"

"I don't know, better ask Dad."

That night when Dad came home I asked him, "What are your vitals Dad?"

Dad repled, "Balls."

I thought that was very rude and I told him so.

"Oh no! No! I mean your vitals are your balls."

Cor! I was supposed to dip my balls in ice water.

After we had recovered from rolling on the floor splitting our sides, I thought, 'No, thank you.' I decided to put my own interpretation, more suitable to our climate, on Mr Atlas's Dynamic Tension Course – I would bathe my vitals in warm water.

I could see that I was getting nowhere at the furniture factory. I didn't want to be gluing wooden reinforcing blocks to table and chair legs forever, so I started walking home by different routes after work, taking in the many side streets around town to see what I could find. One day, as I was wandering around the streets near Smithfield market, I passed this place that had a sign in the window. It said, 'Tailors, machinists, cutters and Hoffman pressers wanted urgently for Ladies mantles and costumes'. The very next day, instead of going to work in the furniture factory, I told Jimmy that I didn't feel well and I was taking the day off. After Mam, Dad and Jimmy had gone off to work and Pat had gone to school, I jumped out of bed, had a bath and then dressed in the suit that I had made at St John's. I brushed my hair, gave my shoes a polish and hurried down to see if I could get a job in the place that I had found the previous day. I set off walking the two miles and planning in my head what I would say. I was wearing this suit to show them what I could do. I didn't think that Ladies mantles and costumes were any different, the stitches and buttonholes are the same, I only hoped that my deafness wouldn't be a problem. I was unaware that there were social workers in the deaf club who would help in cases like this. Anyway, I would rather do it myself and not rely on any hearing person.

By the time I arrived there I wasn't feeling so sure of myself. My confidence was quickly draining away as I stood there hesitating on the street corner. Some people were arriving for work and entering the door. Plucking up courage, I asked one of the men who had a friendly face where did I apply for a job? He said, "Come with me sonny, I'll show you." I followed him down a corridor where we came to a door marked 'Office'. He said, "Just go in there and tell them what you want, you'll be alright." I thanked him for his help and he went off.

It was a few minutes before a young lady opened the office door in answer to my timid knocking. She smiled at me and said, "Yes, can I help you young sir?" I felt myself going red, and I kept swallowing trying to find my voice. At last I managed to stammer that I had come for a job. She must have felt sorry for me as I could see the amusement in her eyes as she told me to take a seat and she would get the manager.

As I sat there I thought, 'Oh! Bloody 'ell, I must have pronounced some words wrong, she was laughing at me. That's torn it, I'll not get a job here now, they'll think I'm retarded, or an escapee from a lunatic asylum.' The young lady came back and gave me an encouraging smile as she returned to her desk, and a few minutes later a small middle aged man came and sat down next to me. He shook my hand and said, "Hello, I'm Mr Weingard, I'm the manager, what can I do for you?" I explained that I had come for a job and I told him that I had made my suit myself and showed him the buttonholes and stitches, and I thought it was best to explain that I was deaf and I was lip reading him because a lot of people didn't like the way I looked directly at their faces when talking. Mr Weingard said not to worry, he knew that I was deaf because he had a brother who was deaf and he could tell. Then he asked me if it would be alright if he put me to work in the cutting room starting the next day. The wages would be three pounds a week, which was not bad for a sixteen year old lad in 1951 – It was 10 shillings more than I was getting at the furniture factory. In those days you could get eight pints of beer and a packet of cigarettes for ten bob, so I said that was OK with me. He then gave me a form to take home to fill in with all my details and bring back the next day.

On the way home I felt better than I had in months. I thought, 'Wow! That was easy.' I didn't realise that I had been lucky and it wasn't always as easy as that. When I started work at 'Northcote and Brewer, Ladies Costumes and Mantles' at 8.30 the next morning I was painfully shy and withdrawn. The people who worked there were very nice and made me welcome, but I still had to make an effort to pluck up courage to answer whenever one of them spoke to me or asked a question. I was wondering if I was speaking correctly all the time and this made me keep the conversations as brief as possible. If it was a woman or girl who spoke to me I could feel myself going red in the face. They must have thought I was being unfriendly, or at least they must have thought I was a very strange young man. I still had a long way to go before I was at ease in the hearing world. We deaf kids had been taught at St John's that the outside world was evil and we must be on our guard at all times lest we be corrupted, and we must be extra careful when dealing with women, who would lead us astray. I knew it was ridiculous because no woman had tried to lead me astray yet (What were they waiting for?) and I knew it was ridiculous when I was told this at St John's by Sister Margaret and Father Ronchetti. Even so, after eight years of that kind of indoctrination some of it must have sunk into my subconscious.

The work in the cutting room was easy. I was put to work cutting the collars and patch pockets of various styles of ladies coats and costumes, so there was a bit of variety. It was more interesting than sticking reinforcing blocks on table legs! I worked with a man named Sam and I got on well with him. There was a deaf man who worked as a presser in the same room and his name was Bill Cawley. We would sit together at dinner time in the canteen and have a conversation in sign. The Manchester signing was very different from Boston Spa signing, so Bill was constantly correcting me. I thought that he was a rather opinionated man, but apart from that I got on with him OK. He never bought dinner in the canteen, nor would he drink tea or coffee; he brought sandwiches made from a heavy stone-milled whole wheat bread and drank hot water. He had a cup and a little tea pot which he would fill with hot water from the geyser in the canteen, whilst I would be stuffing myself with the canteen food, steak pie and suet dumplings followed by two helpings of spotted dick with lashings of custard. He explained to me that my diet was very unhealthy and that horses ate corn and drank water, nothing else, and they were very strong. I said, "Neigh! Your reasoning is flawed. Horses ate grass too. Where is your grass? And they drank cold water. And anyway, we are not horses." I think he was trying to wean me off that unhealthy food, but after the short rations I had been on at St John's he didn't have a chance. I don't think he liked me answering back like that, so I resolved to be kinder in future and not argue with him because he wanted to appear as a wise old man.

The weeks and months passed. I had cut a million collars and patch pockets; King George died and Elizabeth was crowned Queen, which we all gathered at Auntie Ruth's to watch on her new television with the tiny screen and big cabinet. There were crates of beer and lashings of food, just like the old wartime days. Everest was conquered and another far more important incident (to me) occurred one day during dinner time at work. One of the girls came to me and said that there was a deaf and dumb [sic] man who had started work at our place. "Come and see, he's outside talking to another deaf and dumb [sic] man." We looked out of the window at them signing together. Just then, as I was remembering my signing friends and smiling at the memory, this man looked up and saw me looking at him and smiling. He signed to the other man, "Look at them two laughing at us because we are deaf." They were surprised when I signed to them that I was deaf too. He beckoned to me to come down. They were going for a pint in the pub on the corner, so I went to the Hat and Feathers pub with them and we introduced ourselves. His name was Peter Kilgour and we soon became friends. He took me to the deaf club at Grosvenor Street, All Saints, which was across town, and introduced me to everyone. They were a very friendly bunch of people and I soon felt at home with them. Then I was persuaded to join their football and cricket teams.

The signing was different from Boston Spa's but I soon picked it up and made many friends. It was a good feeling to be back in the deaf world again. I would go to the deaf club on Mondays after work and on Saturdays after playing football in those days the deaf people had taken over the All Saints Tavern, which was a small pub round the corner from the deaf club. We had some good times there. Beer from the wooden barrels is far superior to the beer from modern metal barrels and it seemed that I could drink lots more from those wooden barrels than I can now from the metal barrels. Sometimes the old ways are best. I asked about Father Hayward's club and I was given directions on how to get there. I decided that I would go there the following week to see what it was like.

On the Sunday morning I caught the trolley bus into town, then walked up Deansgate until I came to Chester Road. I continued along Chester Road until I came to number 431. I stood outside examining the place for a few minutes. I thought, 'So this is what all the fuss was about, this is the evil place that Sister Teresa warned me to keep away from.' It was just an ordinary mid-terrace Victorian house. There was nothing sinister about it. Maybe inside was different, maybe they were Devil worshippers, let's go and see.

Inside I was made welcome. I recognised some of the people from when they visited St John's and they shook my hand and took me to Father Hayward. He said that he remembered me from St John's and I was very welcome. Father Hayward said Mass in one of the back rooms, which was used as a chapel, and after Mass we all went upstairs for a cup of tea and have a chat and to get to know each other better. I found them very pleasant people and decided to come again. Father Hayward was the first ever deaf Catholic priest and his modest little club and church on Chester Road was the harbinger of signed Masses for the deaf and the CDA (Catholic Deaf Association) all over Britain.

A few weeks later I again went to Chester Road. As I entered the door one of the men, Terry Riley, approached me. He had a twinkle in his eye as he said, "Now, don't go mad, keep calm, just go quietly into that room," he pointed to a room on the left, "and look at the beautiful girl there." I wondered what he was going on about, but when I entered the room and saw her my jaw hit the floor. Terry was looking at me and smiling. Again he said, "Calm down, don't go mad and embarrass the poor girl."

She was surrounded by people all trying to talk to her. Then she turned and looked at me. I don't know if a nightingale sang in Berkeley Square, but I do know that my legs turned to rubber and my life would never be the same again. That was the first time that I saw Diana Taylor. It was one of those moments in your life that you can never forget. Thank you God! Thank you Sister Teresa, I love you!

The next week I plucked up the courage to ask Diana out to the pictures. She shocked me by saying "Yes". From that day I stopped eating those stodgy canteen dinners and saved every penny I had so that I could take Diana out and spend it on her. Meeting Diana changed my life completely, for the better I must add. I cut down on the boozing with Jimmy and his hearing pals. Now it's hard for me to remember what it was like BD (Before Diana). This year will be our 50th wedding anniversary, how about that.

Another week later, with Diana at Chester Road, I met Johnny Glancy. I had heard a lot about him from older lads of St John's. It seems that he was quite a character, and it was good to meet him in the flesh at last. Johnny invited Diana and I to his home in Stockport to meet his wife Eileen. So, one Sunday afternoon, Diana and I made our way to Stockport and found his house. Johnny was only a small man but broad in the chest and shoulders, and strong too, Eileen opened the door and invited us in. Johnny was sitting in an armchair eating ham sandwiches and looking at the pictures in an old 'Playboy' magazine when we entered the room. He quickly slid the Playboy under a stack of 'Health and Strength' magazines, got up and wiped bread crumbs from his mouth, then greeted us and bade us welcome to his humble abode. While Diana and Eileen were getting to know each other after tea, Johnny took me to his gym. He was renting out a room in the back of a pub about half a mile away from his house and he had turned it into a gym with lots of weights, bars, dumbbells, pulleys, benches, etc. He also had about ten members who paid him to train there. I was amazed, I thought it was great, much better than the Charles Atlas course. Johnny was very forward-looking and ahead of his time, because weight training was frowned upon in those days. The 'experts' said that it made you muscle-bound and that your biceps would become so big that you couldn't touch your head. Now I know why that little man holding a comb followed Johnny around.

Johnny gave me the address of a friend of his who lived near me in Middleton. This friend was 'Mr Britain', Ken Latham, so next day I went to see Ken Latham and joined his weightlifting club. He said that "any friend of Johnny Glancy's is a friend of mine too". I learned a lot about how to get strong and how to focus your strength from Ken, so later on, when working in the roofing trade, I was able to use that strength. I could also break six inch nails in twenty seconds and tear phone books just as easily. Anybody who knew me as 'little Fitz' back in the old Collyhurst days wouldn't recognise me now, and so even though I was deaf, I was able to command some respect from the rough and ready blokes who worked on the building sites. I was known as 'Deaf Kev' on these building sites, but when they saw what I could do, that changed to 'Big Kev', even though I was only five foot seven!

In the meantime, our Pat had been courting a lad named Arthur Travis. He emigrated to Canada and Pat decided to follow him. It was a sad day when Mam and I went with her to Liverpool to see her off on the 'Empress of Canada', which was a massive liner. I couldn't believe that our Pat was leaving us, especially for a man like Arthur Travis who I considered a bit of an idiot. He was born and brought up in Levenshulme which is a suburb in Manchester, but he tried to dress like an American. He also sported a crew cut, just like the Yankee soldiers had, and tried to drawl with a Texan accent. He seemed a very shallow man to me and I just couldn't understand what our Pat saw in him. But it was her life and she was 18 years old, so she had my full support.

About this time my Dad became very ill and had to be sent away to a sanatorium. My Mam was struggling to make ends meet and I tried my best to help her, but my wages from the tailor's were not much help, so I decided that I had to find another job with more money. I talked it over with Peter Kilgour at work and he told me that he used to work for a company called the Ruberoid Roofing Company and they paid good wages. While I was earning about £5 a week as a cutter in the rag trade, I could earn more than £15 as a roofer, but the work was hard and dangerous, which is why he had given it up. Those kind of wages made my mind up. He told me that the boss's name was Mr Birtles and where the office was. Next day I went to see Mr Birtles, who told me that they had just started a big job in Trafford Park. It was over 90 feet high and it was expected to last for two years, and he would pay good wages with plenty of overtime. But the work was hard and dangerous and it was hard to get good workers because of that. Was I still interested? I said, "Yes, when do I start? Will next week be OK because I would like to give notice at my current job?" Next day, when I gave my notice that I was leaving, they all told me that I was doing a foolish thing and I would be very sorry. I told them that I had enjoyed working with them and would be sorry to go but I needed to earn more than I was getting there.

So that's how I became a roofer and I was roofing for the next 40 years. The ability to focus and concentrate that I had learned allowed me to overcome my lack of balance caused by my deafness... but that's another story and needs another book.